GOD'S
AMBASSADORS

HUDSON TAYLOR
DAVID LIVINGSTONE
GLADYS AYLWARD
JIM ELLIOT

BARBOUR
PUBLISHING, INC.
Uhrichsville, Ohio

© 2001 by Barbour Publishing, Inc.

ISBN 1-58660-131-8

Hudson Taylor by Susan Martins Miller. © 1993 by Barbour Publishing, Inc.
David Livingstone by Dan Larsen. © 1992 by Barbour Publishing, Inc.
Gladys Aylward by Sam Wellman. © 2001 by Sam Wellman.
Jim Elliot by Susan Martins Miller. © 1998 by Barbour Publishing, Inc.

All Scripture quotations are taken from the King James Version of the Bible.

Published by Barbour Publishing, Inc., P.O. Box 719, Uhrichsville, Ohio 44683
http://www.barbourbooks.com

 Member of the
Evangelical Christian
Publishers Association

Printed in the United States of America.

CONTENTS

HUDSON TAYLOR

PIONEER MISSIONARY IN CHINA

by Susan Martins Miller

CHAPTER 1

The small boy sat very quietly, watching intently. His father gently and precisely measured powders and liquids and set them aside on the counter in his shop.

Hudson Taylor knew that his father had an important job—preparing the medicines that the doctors in Barnsley, England, wanted their patients to take. He also knew that he must not speak while his father was concentrating on the medicines. Still, he loved to watch. From time to time, the bell on the shop door jingled, and someone would come in to pick up a preparation. Hudson looked on proudly as his father gave instructions about how the medicine should be used. Between customers, father and son smiled at each other as if they had a secret known only to them.

Hudson turned his head as he heard a familiar creak and realized that his mother was coming through the door connecting the shop with the family's rooms behind it. The young woman saw her oldest child sitting so contentedly on the stool behind the counter, and she wished she did not have to disturb him. But the two parents had agreed that they would bring up their children to look after their own things and to develop the careful habit of repairing something as soon as it needed attention.

"There you are, Hudson," she said, smiling. "Have you

been out here all afternoon? I never thought a five year old could be so interested in the work of a chemist!"

"I am interested, Mama, and I like to be with Papa." The boy's words were obviously sincere; Hudson's mother smothered a smile of amusement at how such a small child could be so serious.

"I noticed that the underarm seam of your nightshirt is a little loose. I think perhaps you ought to stitch it before it becomes a large hole."

"Must I do it now, Mama?" Hudson pleaded.

"Absolutely. The needle and thread are ready for you on your dressing table. If you need help, I'll be in the sitting room."

Hudson knew that it was pointless to protest further. Mama always insisted that he do these things right away. He hopped down off the stool and started toward his mother. When he heard his father speak, he stopped for a moment to listen.

"I'm glad you came into the shop, Dear," his father said. "I've invited some of the traveling ministers to tea this afternoon. It's been months since we had a good talk with any of them."

"Good! I look forward to visiting with them, too."

Hudson and his brother and sister were only little children, but they loved to listen to the stories the preachers told from their trips all around England and several other countries. Standing in the doorway listening to his parents, he wanted to say how much he enjoyed the visits of the traveling Methodist ministers. Instead, Hudson glanced up at his mother and decided that he should go directly to his room to mend his nightshirt.

He had to stand on his tiptoes to see the top of his dresser and reach for the sewing basket. He carried it carefully to his bed, where he reached under his pillow for his nightshirt. Hudson knew right were the loose seam was; he had seen it for himself two days ago. He climbed up on the high bed, got comfortable right in the middle of it, and began making small, exact stitches in the fabric. As he sewed, he listened to his mother moving about the sitting room preparing for the guests who would be coming soon.

Mama always hid her own mending basket on the empty bottom shelf of the bookcase, behind the ruffled crimson curtain she had hung to brighten the room. The family's home was small, and Mama did not have all the pretty dishes that other mothers had, but Hudson felt very secure living there with his parents and his brother, William, and sister, Amelia. Soon Mama would have another baby, and the rooms would become even more crowded, but Hudson did not mind.

Hudson was nearly finished mending when his sister Amelia, who was only three, came in with the exciting news that the traveling Methodist ministers would be coming to tea soon.

"I know that already," Hudson said, trying to act very old. "Papa told Mama while I was in the shop."

Amelia was clearly disappointed that Hudson had discovered this wonderful news and had not shared it with her immediately. He could see she was unhappy, so he added, "I would have told you right away, but Mama sent me in to mend my nightshirt."

That seemed to make his little sister feel better, and she climbed up on the bed to sit next to him. But she climbed right down again when the shop doorbell jangled and she heard the voices of the guests they were waiting for. Hudson slid off the bed as quickly as he could, tucked his nightshirt under the pillow, returned the sewing basket to the dresser, and eagerly followed Amelia out into the sitting room.

His brother William, four years old, was already sitting quietly in one corner. The three children knew that they must not speak while their guests were talking, but the restriction never seemed to bother them. Papa and Mama would answer all their questions later. Right now, they were content to listen to the adventurous stories the preachers told about the many people who believed in God and became Christians. Some of the men traveled around the country preaching all the time. Others, like Hudson's father, had other jobs to support their families and preached whenever they could. The best stories were from the guests who had been to foreign countries.

The pile of biscuits slowly disappeared, and the tea in the pot grew cold as the friends tried to catch up on all that had happened in the last few months. As he had in other meetings, Hudson's father brought the group's attention to one thing which weighed heavily on his heart.

"I don't know why the Methodists do not send any missionaries to China. There are millions of souls being lost each and every day in that great land. This is 1837, and we still have no Methodist missionaries in China." Papa would shake his head sadly, and others agreed with him. Still, at the next meeting there would be no report from China.

Hudson sat noiselessly until all the guests were gone, but he was very bothered by what his father had said about China. He hardly knew what China was, but he knew it was a very big country where people did not know about God, and this was what troubled his father.

The small boy, only five years old, crossed the room and put his hand on his father's knee. Papa looked at him and said, "Yes, Hudson? Do you have a question?"

"No, Papa, not a question. I just want to say that when I grow up I will be a missionary, and I will go to China."

CHAPTER 2

"Come on, Hudson," George said. "It's quitting time."

"And I'm ready to quit," seventeen-year-old Hudson answered. "My eyes are really tired today." He rubbed both eyes with the heels of his hands, trying to rid them of the constant stinging sensation that had been bothering him for several weeks.

George reached across the desk to turn off the gaslight by which the two young men had been working. "I never thought there would be so much extra work at a bank," George said. "After all, we closed to the public several hours ago."

"Still, I like the work," Hudson said as they walked toward the door by the dim light of the streetlamp outside.

George smiled. "It does you good to get out of your father's shop. He's spent the last seventeen years filling your head with a bunch of silly religious ideas. There is more to the world than Methodist preachers."

Hudson did not reply. It was true that his job as a junior clerk in the Barnsley bank had exposed him to many ideas his father disapproved of, and he had long ago stopped discussing these things with his family. He hated to have a wall in his relationship with his parents; they had always been a close family. Yet he felt the time had come for him to grow up and begin to think for himself. His friends at the bank had helped him to do that. Hudson was stimulated by their long philosophical discussions on politics, morality, and religion. At first he was eager to discuss religion and share his Christian upbringing. Gradually he began to spend more time listening. His new friends said things he had never thought about before, and he realized how sheltered his childhood had been. Perhaps his fellow clerks were right when they sneered at the traditional religious ideas his parents had taught him.

Hudson worked at the bank only a few months. The stinging in his eyes grew into a serious inflammation caused by the gaslights. Dismayed, Hudson had no choice but to resign and go back to working in his father's chemist's shop. Even working with his father, however, did not make Hudson forget the conversations at the bank. He longed to be on his own, to earn his own money and spend his nights with his friends, perhaps even buy a horse to go hunting with them. Despite the effort his parents made to understand him, his discontentment continued.

One afternoon Hudson had a few hours off from his work in the shop and browsed through the books in his father's library looking for something to read. Nothing seemed to interest him until his eyes fell on a basket of pamphlets. He picked one up and flipped through a few pages. *Perhaps there is a good story here,* he thought. *I'll skip the sermon at the end.* He sat down to read the small book without any intention of taking it seriously. He was just looking for a way to pass the time.

But the book was more interesting than he had expected,

and he could not put it down. When the story ended and the sermon began, he kept reading about how the death of Christ on the cross at Calvary provided a full and perfect atonement for sin—even for his own sin. At first Hudson scanned over the paragraphs, telling himself that he had known this since he was a small child.

Suddenly he realized what this meant! If Christ's work was complete and the whole debt paid, what was left for him to do? A light flashed inside Hudson at that moment, and he could not resist the urge to fall to his knees and pray for this complete salvation he was reading about. All those years of instruction from his parents no longer seemed like a lot of silly religious ideas, as his friend George would think. Hudson was convinced that he had come to the end of his search for truth. His mother and father had been right all along and had waited so patiently for him to realize this himself.

As excited as he was, Hudson kept his conversion a secret for several days. His mother was out of town, and he wanted her to be the first to know. But he was so excited, he found it too difficult to keep the news to himself that long, and he confided in his sister, Amelia.

"Oh, Hudson, that's wonderful!" Amelia was truly delighted. "I knew you were struggling to decide what you believed, and I have been praying for you three times a day for a month. I'm so glad to know my prayers have been answered."

"I never knew you were praying, Amelia. Thank you!" Hudson impulsively embraced his sister, grateful for the part she had played in his new faith. "But please don't tell anyone. I want to tell Mother myself when she comes home next week."

When Mrs. Taylor walked through the door two weeks after Hudson's unforgettable day, he greeted her enthusiastically. "I have such glad news to tell you, Mother!"

She reached out and put her arms around his neck and held him close like she used to do when he was small. "I know, my boy," she said simply.

Hudson pulled back, very surprised and disappointed. He had not yet said what his news was. "Has Amelia broken her promise and told you?"

"No, Hudson, it was not from any human source that I found out. Two weeks ago I felt such a burden for your conversion that I got up from the dinner table and locked myself in my room. I was resolved not to leave that room until my prayers were answered. I prayed for hours, and that very day I felt the assurance that at last you knew my Lord for yourself."

The weeks that followed were a joyful time for the Taylor family. Amelia and Hudson went into the poorest parts of town on Sunday evenings to distribute pamphlets which would help others make the discovery Hudson had made that day in his father's library. They spoke with anyone who would listen and prayed for the people they met.

However, Hudson's quest to know the Lord was not over. As the weeks passed and the newness of his faith wore off, he found himself feeling like he would rather sleep late instead of getting up early to read his Bible, and praying seemed like too much effort. Even as he felt this happening, Hudson did not like it. Surely God had more of a purpose for his life than this! He longed to be genuinely close to God, yet he felt unworthy to approach God. He continued to do things he knew were wrong, and the good things he meant to do somehow never got done.

For days and weeks, Hudson could not figure out what was keeping him back. What could he do to rid himself of his sinfulness? He prayed constantly for God to show him what he should do. If only God would break the power of sin and allow Hudson to live a holy life, he would give himself completely to whatever God wanted him to do. If only God would deliver him!

Hudson was startled when he thought he heard someone in the room with him—he had been sure he was alone. The room was dark, and he peered into the shadows to see who had entered. But no one was there. Hudson caught his breath as he realized that the presence he felt was God's presence. As he sat in awe, he heard his prayer being answered as if God were speaking in a human voice. "Your prayer is answered. I will deliver you. Then go for Me to China."

The young man, now seventeen, had long ago forgotten his childhood declaration that he would go to China. It was at this dramatic moment, during his unusual and spectacular meeting with God, that Hudson Taylor was convinced that he would go to China as a missionary. This was the meaning of his months of spiritual struggle—to prepare him to say "Yes" to God's call. From that hour his mind was made up. Everything he did from that time on was to prepare him for the work God wanted him to do.

CHAPTER 3

Hudson Taylor wasted no time getting ready to go to China. Immediately he decided to go beyond the chemist trade he had learned from his father and study medicine and go to China as a missionary doctor. He longed to go as soon as possible, but he knew he must be fully prepared.

He sat in the lecture hall during the day and pored over his medical books at night, pondering being a doctor in a foreign country. He would be far from his family, living in a land of strange traditions and a complicated language, thousands of miles away from anyone who would provide support for him. Though he had not yet been to China, he had read about the country and often tried to picture himself living among the people of that great land. He soon began to study the Chinese language in the leisure hours he had and to learn as much about the country as he could.

Hudson was still not satisfied that he was ready to go to China. He could prepare his mind by studying medicine and the Chinese language. He could prepare his body by maintaining good health. But he must also be prepared spiritually. Hudson was confident that God was able to provide whatever he needed at just the time that he needed it. His doubts were not about God but about himself. Did he have enough faith to trust God completely? During these years of preparation for a lifelong commitment to China, this was a serious question in his mind.

Hudson was so hounded by this question that he looked for ways to test his own faith even while he was still living in England. He began working for a doctor as part of his training. When they first met, Dr. Hardey said to Hudson, "I will pay your salary every three months. But you must remind me when it is due, because I am very forgetful and probably will not remember on time."

With a silent nod and a lump in his throat, Hudson recognized that here was an opportunity to test his faith. He decided right then that he would not remind Dr. Hardey when it was time for him to be paid. Instead he would pray that the doctor would remember. If Dr. Hardey forgot to pay him, then Hudson would trust God to provide the money he needed another way.

After several months, Hudson was due to be paid, but Dr. Hardey made no mention of his salary. Hudson stuck to his resolution and did not remind the doctor. Days passed, and Hudson found himself down to his last coin one Saturday night. This small amount was all the money he would have until Monday, when perhaps Dr. Hardey would remember to pay him. Hudson was not concerned. He always seemed to have what he needed, so he continued praying and thanking God for being faithful.

On Sunday evening of that weekend, Hudson was out distributing pamphlets in a very poor section of town. A ragged,

weary man approached him and asked Hudson to come home
with him and pray for his dying wife. He followed the man
into his small, dark room, where he saw five children huddled
in one corner, their cheeks sunken and their eyes blank. It was
clear that they were slowly starving to death. The man's wife
was lying on a pallet on the floor with a newborn baby at her
side, both of them obviously dying.

Hudson choked back tears as he looked around at this
miserable family. As the children looked on, he took the woman's hand and began to pray for her. As he struggled for
words, he could almost feel the only coin he had burning
a hole in his pocket. If only he had several coins, he would
gladly give them most of the money. As it was, he would have
to give them everything he had or give them nothing.

The man had asked him to pray, so Hudson started praying. But his words were disconnected and made no sense, even
to Hudson. Finally the man broke in and said, "You see what a
terrible state we are in, Sir. If you can help us, please do!"

At that moment the words flashed into Hudson's mind,
Give to the one who asks of you. Slowly he reached into his
pocket and closed his hand around his coin. He pulled it out
and placed it in the man's hand. It was not a great deal of
money, but he explained that it was all he had. The man was
very grateful, for even a small amount of money would en-
able him to call the doctor to come and help his wife.

The next morning, Monday, Hudson ate the last of the
porridge he had on hand. He had no more food in the house,

no more money in his pocket, and no guarantee that Dr. Hardey would remember to pay him. As he thought about his problem, he heard a knock on the door and was surprised when his landlady brought in a letter. Hudson was puzzled. He did not recognize the handwriting on the envelope, and the postmark had been smudged, so he could not tell where the letter had come from. Swiftly he slit the corner of the envelope and reached in. Still puzzled, he unfolded the sheet of paper—only to find it was blank. However, wrapped inside the paper was some money—much more money than he had given away the night before. In all the years that followed, Hudson never knew who sent that package to him.

At least now he knew he would be able to buy food for a few more days. But there was still the problem that Dr. Hardey had not remembered to pay him. Each day of that week, Hudson struggled to keep his promise not to remind the doctor but only to pray for God to remind him. Over and over again, he told himself that if he could not withstand this test of his faith, then he was not ready to go to China.

By Saturday Hudson was beginning to feel embarrassed. Not only was he out of food again, but his landlady would be expecting a rent payment. If he did not pay his rent, then she could not buy the things she needed for herself. The day crept by slowly. Hour by hour, Hudson prayed silently for Dr. Hardey to remember his salary.

Finally, late in the afternoon, Dr. Hardey said, "By the way, Taylor, is not your salary due again?"

Hudson was overcome with emotion. The doctor had remembered! He found that he had to swallow several times before he could even respond to the doctor. Keeping busy and looking away from Dr. Hardy, he said, "It has been overdue for some time now, Sir." He felt such relief that his prayer had been answered he could hardly speak.

"Oh, I am sorry that you did not remind me! You know how busy I am. I wish I had thought of it a little sooner, for only this afternoon I sent all the money I had to the bank. Otherwise I would pay you at once."

Hudson could hardly believe his ears. He was not going to be paid, after all! Once again he swallowed hard and tried to control his emotions. His hand shook as he lifted some supplies off the counter, and he concentrated very hard on not letting Dr. Hardey see how upset he was. Seeming calm outwardly and trying to appear as normal as possible, he slowly walked from the room.

When he returned to the room, Dr. Hardey had left for the evening. Hudson sat down on a stool and let his shoulders sag. Should he have given in to the urge to remind Dr. Hardey to pay him? Was it fair to make his landlady suffer because he wanted to practice believing God? Confused, Hudson sat alone in the dark, praying for the right decision.

At ten o'clock that night, still with no clear answer in his mind, Hudson was ready to put out the light and go home. With his overcoat halfway on, he heard a noise and stopped to listen carefully. Dr Hardey was walking very quickly—he was laughing aloud. He burst into the room with a grin on his face and explained to the puzzled young man, "One of my wealthiest patients just came by to pay his bill. I do not know what prompted him to come at this hour, but he has paid in cash. Here, take part of the money to tide you over, and I will pay you the rest of your salary next week."

He was gone as quickly as he had come. Hudson stood in the doorway with his fingers wrapped around the bills the doctor had pressed into his hand. Standing alone in the dark, he said aloud, "I will be able to go to China, after all."

CHAPTER 4

"September 19, 1853." Hudson Taylor, now twenty-one years old, wrote the date very carefully in his journal and described in detail all that had happened on that day. He was sailing for China at last.

He was finally able to answer fully God's call for him to take the gospel to China. Although he had not quite finished his medical degree and had not been ordained, the Chinese Evangelization Society had felt he was ready to go to China as a missionary. On that early fall morning he boarded the *Dumfries,* a cargo ship, as the only passenger.

His full heart almost broke at the sight of his mother standing on the pier waving good-bye. She had come aboard to be sure his cabin was adequate, and together they had sung a hymn and knelt in prayer. And then she had returned to the pier while he remained on board. Not until the very moment of parting from his family did Hudson understand the price they were all paying by his obedience to God's call.

After the ship lurched away from the dock, Hudson closed his diary and looked around his small cabin. Being a passenger on a cargo ship was the least expensive way to get to China; it was not the fastest nor the most comfortable. The captain had told him the voyage could take as long as six months, and this confining space where Hudson now sat would be his home for that time.

He decided to go up on deck and watch the land slide from his sight. In the quiet moments while he was leaning over the rail, he felt God's comfort and was confident he had made the right choice in going to China at this time.

Unfortunately, the winds were not right for making progress with great speed. The *Dumfries* spent more than a week in the English Channel, trying to make its way out to open sea. Finally, on the twelfth frustrating day the winds suddenly picked up. At first Hudson thought this was a good sign and was excited that his journey would at last be underway. But soon he realized that the captain was not as pleased with the increasing winds. Something was definitely wrong. Hudson watched as the able crew moved swiftly about the deck trying to capture the power of the wind. The sails flapped loudly as the muscular men pulled on the ropes and followed the orders shouted by the captain.

Soon it was clear that everyone on board was in serious danger. When Hudson saw the captain running across the deck toward the mainsail, he grabbed his arm and tried to stop him.

"Sir, please tell me what I can do to help!"

"Just stay out of the way, young man!" The captain roughly shrugged off Hudson's touch and sprinted once again toward the crew.

As Hudson stood watching, frustrated that he could not help, he lost his balance and nearly went over the rail. Rather than sending the ship out into the open sea, the wind, blowing at gale force, was moving the *Dumfries* toward a formation of huge rocks close to the coast. Enormous waves beat viciously against the side of the vessel, rocking it from side to side.

Hudson gripped the railing tightly now. He had seen the rocks for himself and understood the danger which threatened everyone. Ducking his head against the wind and pulling himself along the railing with two hands, he made his way toward the stairs which would take him down to his cabin. Once there, sheltered from the wind but still swaying from side to side, he managed to write out his name and address and put the small piece of paper in his pocket. His hope was that when his body was found there would be someone who could notify his family. Then he searched through his belongings for things that might float and tied these things together into a bundle.

Just as he did so, resigned to his own death without seeing China, the swaying seemed to slow down. Hudson felt the ship change direction; he grabbed his bundle and ran up the stairs to see what was going on. What he saw horrified him. They were nearly upon the treacherous rocks, yet the captain continued to try to turn the boat around—and was succeeding at last. In a few more minutes the turn was complete, and captain and crew began to relax. A victorious shout went up from the men when they were sure that they were out of danger.

The journey continued smoothly for many weeks after that perilous beginning. Hudson discovered that there was a Swedish carpenter on board who was also a Christian, and together they held regular worship services for the crew. By the time they reached New Guinea, two others had become Christians.

It was during a service off the coast of New Guinea that Hudson saw the captain repeatedly looking over the rail with an expression of concern. When Hudson asked the reason for his worried look, the captain explained that the vessel was being carried toward sunken reefs that could destroy the ship and again endanger the lives of the crew. Using all his skill, the captain did everything he could to avoid the reef, but at last he told Hudson there was nothing more to do.

"But, Captain, there is more we can do." Seeing the captain's puzzled face, the young missionary continued. "There are four of us on board who are Christians. We will go to our cabins and pray for God's help."

"It can do no harm, Mr. Taylor. Do as you wish." The captain certainly expected nothing to come of their prayers, but he thought that the Christians might as well go to their deaths believing in their God.

Hudson and the three others did go to pray, each to his own cabin. But Hudson did not stay there long. After only a few minutes of prayer, he was convinced that God would save the ship. He dashed back up on the deck and saw the first officer sitting at the base of the mainsail. There was absolutely no wind, and the ship was drifting ever closer to the threatening reefs.

"Sir!" Hudson cried out. "I beg you, let down the mainsail. Let the wind carry us out of danger."

"Are you mad, Mr. Taylor?" the unbelieving officer asked.

"There is no wind. There is no point in letting down the sail."

At that moment the corner of the sail began to flap in response to a gentle breeze. Hearing the sound, the first officer jumped up and immediately began working the mainsail. Other members of the crew hurried to help. Soon the wind grew strong and steady, and the *Dumfries* was on its way back out to the safety of the open sea.

Hudson stood on the deck watching the flurry of activity and gave a prayer of thanks. Surely this faithful God would deliver him safely to the shore of China and generously provide for every need he faced in the task of preaching the gospel to the Chinese people.

CHAPTER 5

Hudson stood before the gate to the missionary compound, where all the missionaries lived and worked, with one bag tucked under his arm and another slung over his shoulder. His heart was beating rapidly as he scanned the outside of the compound. This was the beginning of a whole new way of life for Hudson Taylor. Six months on the boat had made him very anxious to be here, but still he could hardly believe that he had actually arrived in China.

He had just walked more than a mile through the narrow, crowded streets of Shanghai and could hardly believe that he had made his way safely here with his limited understanding of Chinese. Many people in the streets had stopped to look at the strange Englishman who did not know where he was going. But at last he had found his way.

The tall spire of the chapel was the first thing Hudson saw that told him he was in the right place. Standing at the gate now, he could see that there was also a hospital and several houses. He hoped to find Dr. Medhurst, a famous and important missionary in China, and that Dr. Medhurst would be able to help him find a place to live and get started on his work.

Shyly, Hudson knocked on the door of the first house. He had spent six months on a voyage bringing him thousands of miles to this place, yet he was nervous about introducing himself to these people.

Hudson soon found that he did not need to be nervous. The door was quickly opened, and the missionaries graciously welcomed him. For many months, it was difficult to find a house to live in on his own, so he lived with other missionaries, learning about the Chinese way of doing things. Although he had studied the Chinese language while he lived in England, Hudson needed to learn a great deal more before he would be able to live and work among the Chinese people the way he wanted to. Hour after hour, he sat at the table in his room studying Chinese.

The other missionaries in the compound, although kind to Hudson, were very busy with their own work. Sometimes it was hard to concentrate in his room when he wanted to be out doing the work he had come so far from home to do. Hudson could hear the missionaries chattering in Chinese and see them walking up and down the streets with confidence and ease. He strained to listen carefully whenever he heard Chinese being spoken, struggling to make sense of the many complicated sounds which made up the language. Someday, he reminded himself, he would be ready to move about freely and confidently the way they did.

The beginning of Hudson Taylor's missionary work was also difficult because of political events in China. Soldiers were in the streets constantly, firing shots throughout the day as fighting broke out between those who supported the government and those who wanted to change it. Hudson was discouraged each day to look out his window or take a short walk and see the misery of the people around him. Soldiers of both armies tortured each other and stole food and supplies from anyone who had them.

Hudson was in a perplexing and frustrating situation. He wanted to do medical work, but he had not finished his medical training, so he was not truly a doctor. He was used to preaching and praying for others, but he was not really trained as a pastor, either. And the Chinese Evangelization Society, which had sent him to China, had not estimated very well what his expenses would be, and Hudson had almost no money to live on and no idea where he could get more. He had many, many opportunities to test the strength of his faith and to trust God to provide for him during these first lonely months in Shanghai.

At last an invitation came from another missionary for Hudson to go on an evangelistic trip. Hudson and Mr. Edkins set out on a Chinese houseboat for a week's journey. The anchors were drawn up and the sails hoisted and, with the help of the Chinese family who owned the boat, the two missionaries floated down the river, traveling forty miles south of Shanghai.

This was Hudson's first chance to really be out with the Chinese people, to see how they lived, to share in their lives. Although it was only for seven days, he was very excited and enthusiastically handed out Chinese literature throughout the city of Sungkiang.

Before leaving the city, Hudson and Mr. Edkins approached the massive gray pagoda of the Buddhist religion. The enormous structure had stood in the spot for nine hundred years. The priest in charge allowed them to enter the pagoda, and they climbed to a high point where they could look down on the entire city sprawled out below. Tears came to Hudson's eyes as he gazed out on the countryside. From this spot he could see literally thousands and thousands of homes of Chinese people where little was known about Jesus Christ. The villages and temples and cities stretched out before him, calling him once again to go live among the people, to care for their physical needs, and to tell them of the love of God. He remembered the day when he had heard God say, "Then go for Me to China." Silently Hudson scolded himself for the depression and discouragement he had been feeling. God had called him here for a purpose, and standing here at the top of a Buddhist pagoda, he once again felt the Lord's touch gently steering him toward the Chinese people.

Back in Shanghai, Hudson intensified his efforts at language study. Now that he had been out on one evangelistic trip, he was more eager than ever to travel to other places in China with Christian literature and to look for chances to talk to Chinese people. Before long, Hudson was making regular trips to other ports along the coast, sometimes alone, sometimes with another missionary. More and more he saw that the ointments, powders, and pills he carried in his medicine chest were a way to capture the interest of the Chinese, who would then accept his pamphlets and small books, as well. Over and over again he was overwhelmed by the enormous population of China—millions of souls waiting to hear about Jesus Christ.

By the end of his first year in China, Shanghai was at peace once again, and the coastal area had become a comfortable place to continue missionary work. But Hudson was not satisfied. His eyes and heart turned toward the inland parts of China, away from the protected seaports. His soul burned with the burden of reaching these people, and he knew he could not rest until they, too, had received the Christian message.

CHAPTER 6

"She's so beautiful!" Hudson said, looking fondly at the gentle Maria Dyer as she gracefully served tea to the group of missionaries gathered in the city of Ningpo. He did not realize he had spoken aloud until his companion gave him a strange look. Abruptly, Hudson excused himself and drifted off to another part of the house where he could be alone with his thoughts.

For weeks he had been torn in two by his feelings for this lovely young girl. He had no proper home, practically no income, and a career which would demand sacrifice and hardship year after year. What right did he have to think of marriage at this time in his life? What right did he have to think Maria would even consider his offer? Despite everything, however, he loved her more and more every day and dreamed of telling her so. But he never had a chance to express his feelings. Although they met often in a group with other missionaries, Maria and Hudson rarely were alone together.

Slowly Hudson shuffled his feet back to the room where the group was drinking tea and sharing information about their work. When he reached the doorway he stood still, completely captivated by Maria's gliding steps and soft smiles.

After being in Ningpo for only three months, Hudson was called back to Shanghai. Certainly he would have preferred to

GOD'S AMBASSADORS

stay in Ningpo and be near Maria, but he was needed in Shanghai. His new work gave him many opportunities for preaching in several places. While he was glad to be able to do this, Hudson was more lonely every week, missing Maria more all the time. After more than four months, he decided to write to her and ask Maria Dyer to be his wife.

Hudson could hardly concentrate on his work as he waited for her response. The days passed slowly, and more than a week went by. At last, after two weeks, Maria's letter arrived— in an envelope marked with the clear, pretty handwriting which he knew was hers. It was very brief:

> *Dear Mr. Taylor,*
> *I am afraid that what you have suggested is completely impossible. If you have any gentlemanly feeling, then I know you will refrain from troubling me on this subject ever again.*
> *Maria Dyer*

When Hudson read these harsh words, he fell into a chair, stunned. There was no doubt that this was Maria's handwriting, but he could not believe that these were her words! Although they had not had very many chances to be together privately, he had felt sure that she was as fond of him as he was of her. How could this be? Hudson was devastated and bewildered as he read the short letter over and over again, searching for some understanding of why she would write to him in such a curt tone.

His questions went unanswered. His heart ached as he continued to preach in Shanghai. As the months passed, his love for Maria never diminished, and it was with mixed feelings that he responded to a call to return to Ningpo. He could be near Maria, but it might make his heartache worse to be near her and not be able to speak to her. Would he ever know the reason she thought it was impossible for them to marry?

The first time Hudson saw Maria again in Ningpo she smiled sweetly and welcomed him back. "I'm so glad that you have returned to Ningpo," she said. "I trust you have been well during your time in Shanghai."

Hudson was so startled that she had even spoken to him that he stuttered before finally saying, "Yes, Miss Dyer, I have been well. Thank you." Maria's companion touched her elbow and hurried her along, but Hudson could not help but notice that as she walked away she looked over her shoulder at him. Her face looked kind and gentle as always, with no hint of the harsh tone of her letter. Now he was truly puzzled.

Soon the mystery unraveled. The missionary grapevine buzzed with speculation about what was going on between Hudson and Maria, and it was not long before Hudson learned, to his great joy, that Maria had been thrilled with his letter of proposal. However, the director of the school where she worked considered Hudson unworthy of Maria and had instructed her to write the letter Hudson had received. All these months, while Hudson was in Shanghai longing to be with Maria, she was in Ningpo hoping that he would return.

One sultry afternoon in July, Hudson entered the house of a friend and discovered that Maria was also present. Hudson and Maria smiled secretly at one another as they realized that their friends had arranged for them to see one another. On the spur of the moment, Hudson decided that he would waste no time finding out how she felt about him.

"Miss Dyer," he began, "I wanted to ask you. . ." Although he had rehearsed the words over and over in his head, Hudson found it difficult to speak.

"Yes, Mr. Hudson?" Maria said, looking at him coyly with a hint of encouragement in her voice.

Hudson had learned that Maria had an uncle in England who would have to give permission before they could marry, and he had intended only to ask if he might write to her uncle. However, he wanted to know so much more from Maria.

"Miss Dyer. Maria. I love you. I have loved you for a long time, and I want to marry you!"

Now he had said it. As they sat face-to-face, he hoped she could give him an honest answer. Maria was smiling, but she was silent. Breaking out in laughter, Hudson realized he had not yet asked her if she would marry him.

"Miss Dyer, will you consent to be my wife?"

"Mr. Taylor, that would give me great pleasure."

They grinned broadly at each other, hardly aware that there were others in the room. All of the misconceptions of the past few months spilled out as they were joyously reunited. Maria gladly agreed that Hudson should write her uncle in England. They would wait together for the four months it would take for a response to reach them.

On January 20, 1858, a day filled with brilliant sunshine in Ningpo, China, Maria Dyer and Hudson Taylor were married. Hudson wore traditional Chinese clothes, and Maria wore a simple gray silk gown and wedding veil. At long last their prayers were answered, and their hearts were full of gratitude to God.

Two and one-half years after their wedding, after seven years in China, Hudson was exhausted, and his health was poor. Maria and Hudson decided it was time to take their little daughter, Gracie, and return to England for physical rest. While they were there, they would also try to find more missionaries willing to go to China.

When Hudson and Maria stored away their meager worldly goods, bundled up little Gracie, and boarded the ship headed for England in 1860, they had no idea it would be nearly six years before they returned to their beloved China. As delighted as they were to be among friends and family in England, their thoughts and hearts were always far away in Shanghai and Ningpo and other places where their work had taken them. They had come home to England to refresh their health and to appeal to others to join them in their work. Without any hard feelings on either side, Hudson had separated from the Chinese Evangelization Society which had originally sent him to China. The society, with its strict procedures and limitations, confined itself to the coastal towns of China. The burden burning in the hearts of Hudson and Maria was to evangelize the inland areas of that great country.

Their time in England was well spent. Together with a Chinese Christian who had accompanied them on their voyage, Hudson worked on a revision of the Chinese New Testament. He was also invited to write various articles about China and its needs. He was very glad to do this since his articles and the talks he gave would surely interest others in the work being left undone in China. During these years, five workers were recruited and sailed for China, even though the Taylors could not yet return themselves. Hudson and Maria also added three little sons to their family during these years.

Despite progress in all these areas, in 1865, after being in England for five long years, Hudson was discouraged, wondering if there would ever be enough missionaries for China. Rather than increasing, the number of Protestant missionaries in China was dropping every year, and those who were there generally stayed close to the coastal towns. Very few ventured into the heart of the country.

Maria could only stand by and watch her husband withdraw. She tried to let him know in quiet ways that she would gladly listen if he wanted to talk, but he only seemed to keep to himself more and more. For several months, he slept only an hour at a time during the night. Maria tried to keep the four small children from bothering their papa too much, and she continued the family's routine as cheerfully as possible.

When the invitation came for them to spend time at Brighton, a sea town, Maria was delighted. Surely this was just what Hudson needed!

As soon as they arrived at Brighton, little Gracie ran squealing across the sand. "Papa! Papa! Take me to play in the water! Please! Please!"

Hudson could not help smiling down at his adorable daughter. But he did not feel ready to play in the water with the children. He stroked her fine hair as he explained, "We'll have plenty of time for that, Gracie. Right now, Papa wants to take a walk by himself. Would that be all right?"

It was a bright Sunday morning when Hudson yanked off his shoes and socks, rolled up his pants, and let the sand ooze between his toes and then be washed away by the gentle tide pulling back out to sea. It was a perfect, peaceful picture— except that Hudson did not feel peaceful. Even coming to Brighton had not eased his inner torment. His steps quickened, and he began to run along the edge of the water.

Over and over again, he reminded himself that he had no funds to support the missionaries he wanted to send to China. If he asked people to go, they would face danger and perhaps starvation. Was that fair?

He knew he was too ill to try to run in the sand. Maria would surely scold him if she saw him. Yet he kept moving, his thoughts churning and swirling constantly. Even if the missionaries did die of starvation, they would go straight to heaven, and if just one Chinese was saved, wouldn't that be worth the sacrifice? But could he really ask missionaries to make that sacrifice?

Exhausted, Hudson sank down in the sand and rested against a piece of driftwood. The sun was shining brilliantly, and he closed his eyes and leaned his head back. The warmth of the day seeped into his skin, and he almost felt that he could give in to his desperate need of sleep.

Suddenly he sat bolt upright. If these missionaries went to China, it would not be because Hudson Taylor asked them to go. It would be because God Himself asked them to go. Sitting in the sand with no one to hear him, Hudson said aloud, "Why, if we are obeying the Lord, the responsibility rests with Him, not with us!"

He raised his hands and looked to the sky. "The burden is Yours, Lord! As Your servant, I will continue to work, leaving the results to You!"

Hudson now felt immense relief. The burden was no longer on his shoulders—it never had been! The five missionaries whom he had sent to China were doing the work of the Lord, not the work of Hudson Taylor. The conviction he felt about evangelizing inland China was a conviction from God Himself.

With the ocean waves breaking at his feet and the sun beaming down on his shoulders, Hudson took a pencil and his Bible from his pocket. He found a clean spot in the margin and wrote simply, "Prayed for twenty-four willing, skillful laborers at Brighton, June 25, 1865." Twenty-four new missionaries, including those recently gone to China, would work in teams of two to reach the remote parts of the country.

With renewed energy, Hudson took long strides in the sand toward the house at Brighton where his family and friends were waiting for him. When Maria saw him coming, she knew immediately that something tremendously important had happened. They stayed up long into the night talking in excited, hushed voices about what this experience would mean for their family and for the work in China.

First thing in the morning, Hudson went into London and, with a small deposit, opened a bank account in the name of China Inland Mission.

Maria and Hudson stayed in England for almost another year, spurred on by their goal of returning to China with enough teams to reach into the inner areas rather than staying in the safety of the coast. Hudson completed work on an influential book, *China's Spiritual Needs and Claims,* which attracted many people to his cause. The bank account, opened in such a humble manner, grew through generous contributions at a rate more rapid than anyone could have imagined.

On May 26, 1866, the Taylors and their four children were accompanied by one married couple, five single men, and nine single women when they boarded the ship called the *Lammermuir* and sailed once again for China.

The China Inland Mission had been born of faith on a sunny Brighton day.

CHAPTER 8

Hudson and Maria returned to China with great dreams and a driving desire to tell the people of inland China about Jesus Christ. They set up the offices of the new China Inland Mission in their own home and settled the missionaries who had sailed with them into various provinces around the country. The mission work was on the threshold of a new area.

The early years of the mission were difficult years for the Taylors, however. By the summer of 1867, the thermometer frequently read over one hundred degrees, even inside the house. The children were cranky and became sick easily. Maria took the children for a rest in the cooler countryside, and for awhile it seemed they were all better. But then little Gracie, their oldest child, grew ill and began to get weaker each day.

Hudson sat at her bedside, gazing down on his precious daughter and stroking her hot forehead. When at last she fell asleep, Hudson picked up pen and paper and wrote a letter to a friend in England who was supporting his missionary work. He could not help but pour out his heart to his friend, writing:

I am striving to write a few lines from the side of a couch on which my darling Gracie lies dying. Yet God is faithful and strong, and we depend on Him.

In only a few days, Gracie died. Wracked with grief, Hudson wrote to his mother:

Our dear little Gracie! How we miss her sweet voice in the morning, one of the first sounds to greet us when we woke. Is it possible that I shall never again feel the pressure of that little hand, nevermore hear the sweet prattle of those dear lips, nevermore see the sparkle of those bright eyes? Yet I know she is with Jesus and would not wish her back with us.

Maria and Hudson laid their sweet daughter to rest, rejoicing that she was now with Jesus. Casting aside any thought of being discouraged because of their loss, they threw themselves into the work of the China Inland Mission.

Just two years later, it became clear that the heat was again a threat to the health of the children.

"Hudson," Maria said, "we must decide what to do about the children. We dare not risk another summer here for them."

Hudson shook his head sadly. "Yes, I know. Little Samuel especially is very delicate. We must send them back to England."

"I know you are right, Dear," Maria said with a catch in her voice. "Samuel is only five years old. How will we bear being apart from our children?"

Hudson put his arms around his wife and stroked her soft hair. "Our children are a gift from God. He has called us to this work in China, but we must also do what is best for them." Maria nodded silently as her husband continued: "Emily Blatchley has volunteered to return to England with the children so that you can remain here with me."

Maria looked up at Hudson and tried to smile. "I will be so much happier knowing they are with Emily." She wiped away a tear. "But Charles is too little to send. He should stay here with us."

"Then it's settled," Hudson said with determination. "I'll talk to Emily tomorrow."

As the time grew nearer for the four oldest children to return to England, Samuel fell ill. Once again Maria and Hudson looked on, helpless to heal their beloved son, trying only to keep him comfortable. It was only a matter of days before he fell into a deep sleep from which he did not awaken.

The summer brought more than intense heat. China was facing another political crisis with the threat of imminent war. Sickness ravaged many of the missionary families, and Maria insisted on pressing on alone—past the soldiers—to reach one family where death was near. Having suffered the loss of two of her own children, her heart reached out to the young missionaries as she nursed them and prayed for them to return to health. Satisfied that they would get well, she returned to Hudson and their small son, Charles, where she received the good news that her other children had reached England safely.

Soon after this, Maria herself fell ill with cholera. As she lay in her bed, she would imagine the children taking cool, green walks around the pleasant lake in England where they were living. At the peak of the July heat, Maria gave birth to another son, and she welcomed him with great joy and love. However, she was so weak from her own illness that she could not feed the new little one. Soon the baby was sick, too. After only one brief week of life, during which he gave great joy to his mother, tragedy once again struck the Taylor family, and the child died.

Weak as she was, Maria chose the hymns she wanted to be sung at the little funeral. No one guessed how gravely ill Maria really was as she stood at the grave. As soon as the service ended, she went back to bed to try to recover her strength.

Hudson sat by her bedside constantly. She did not seem to be in pain, but Maria was extremely weak and tired and was showing no signs of improvement. As she grew worse, Hudson stayed with her all night, and as the new morning dawned he could see what the darkness had hidden—Maria was very near death. As he realized this, he could feel his own heart tearing.

"My darling," he said, "do you know that you are dying?"

"Dying!" she replied. "What makes you think so?"

Hudson could hardly speak, but he felt he must go on. "I can see it, Darling. Your strength is giving way."

"But I feel no pain, only weariness."

"You are going home, Maria. You will soon be with Jesus."

"I am so sorry," she said softly.

Hudson spoke even more gently now. "Surely you are not

sorry to go to be with Jesus."

"Oh, no! It is not that. You know, Darling, that for ten years there has not been a cloud between me and my Savior. I cannot be sorry to go to Him. But it does grieve me to leave you alone at such a time."

Maria and Hudson spoke few words after that. Having accepted that the end was near, they simply sat together as she drifted into unconsciousness. When the summer sun rose higher, Hudson heard the sounds of the city, coming to life for another day, contrast with Maria's labored breathing. Just after nine o'clock in the morning, she stopped breathing. Though he truly believed that she was at rest in the arms of Jesus now, he was stabbed with the pain of loneliness and silence. In only three short years, he had witnessed the deaths of his daughter, his two sons, and now his beloved Maria. His older children were thousands of miles away in England, and he was left alone in China with motherless little Charles.

Many people would have understood if Hudson Taylor had decided to leave China and return to England permanently. Surely he had sacrificed enough for this enormous country. Yet Hudson never wavered in his conviction that God had called him to China and that there was still a great deal of work that God meant for him to do. Even though his heart ached intensely for his wife, who had been his companion worker, he never let go of his dream for inland China. Instead, it intensified. He wanted to press on with the vision he had shared with Maria—to take Christ into the very heart of China.

CHAPTER 9

The year 1870 had been a very dark time in Hudson Taylor's personal life. Even amid tragedy after tragedy, he pressed on in his work with the China Inland Mission. After twelve years of understanding companionship, he missed Maria every day. He also missed his three older children who were living in England. Late in 1871, Hudson decided he would visit England to attend to some business for the struggling China Inland Mission and to be with his children. He arranged to travel on a steamer and looked forward to some peaceful weeks of meditation and quiet thinking on the open seas.

He stood on the deck of the ship one day early in the voyage, watching the wake churn and foam as the boat hummed along. Lost in thought, he was hardly aware of the other passengers as they passed by chattering and gesturing in their own conversations.

"Mr. Taylor! Why, Mr. Taylor, I had no idea you would be traveling on this ship."

Surprised to hear his name, Hudson turned and looked up at the familiar young face with a friendly smile. "Miss Faulding, what a pleasant surprise. I thought you had left for England several weeks ago." Jennie Faulding had been a friend to Maria and Hudson for many years as they worked with the common goal of spreading the gospel in China.

"I am due for a few months in England, but the work in Hangchow delayed my departure unexpectedly. Are you going home to see your children?"

"Yes, and to look after some Mission business. It will be a delight to share the voyage with such a good friend as you have been."

Jennie and Hudson were together much of the time during the next weeks. They strolled around the deck for exercise, shared a table at mealtime, sat together for long, quiet talks, and sometimes simply enjoyed a comfortable silence between them. They had been friends in China for many years, and now their friendship ripened into love. By the end of the voyage, they had decided to be married as soon as possible.

The new Mrs. Taylor shared the intensity of Hudson's devotion to inland China. During their months in England, they often sat before a large map of China in their living room and prayed and planned for penetrating the interior of China. There were millions of Chinese who had never heard of Christ: They must be reached! Hudson and Jennie met with others who were interested in the work of the China Inland Mission, and established a council which would manage the daily business of the Mission in England, handling financial donations and interviewing people interested in being missionaries to China. Jennie and Hudson were able to return to China with a sense that the Mission was being well taken care of in England.

"I have been looking forward to this trip for a very long time, Mr. Judd," Hudson said to his companion. "We have achieved our goal of establishing a center in Wuchang; now we have an opening into western China." The two missionaries were walking down the ship's ramp. Hudson wanted to make one last check on Mr. Judd's living quarters before leaving him to handle the work in Wuchang on his own.

"Watch out, Mr. Taylor!" shouted Mr. Judd. But it was too late. Hudson lost his footing and lay sprawled on the ramp looking stunned and embarrassed.

"Are you all right, Sir? Perhaps you ought not to move just yet."

Hudson looked up into the anxious face of his friend and tried to put him at ease.

"I'm sure I'm quite fine, Mr. Judd. I seem to have twisted my ankle a little; that is all. Why don't you help me up and we'll see about it?"

Mr. Judd locked his arms around Hudson and lifted him gently to his feet. Hudson began to wince immediately and hopped on one foot. "Perhaps we had better find a place to sit down, Mr. Judd."

They moved together over to a crate and Hudson sat down. Reluctantly, Hudson admitted his pain. "Perhaps you should go find the ship's doctor."

The sudden fall on the gangplank had serious consequences. In addition to the injured ankle, Hudson experienced severe back pain and could move around only with the aid of crutches. Two months later, while he was still in great pain, news reached him that Miss Emily Blatchley, who was taking care of his children and looking after the Mission in England, had died. Despite his deteriorating physical condition, Jennie and Hudson set out for England immediately.

In England, Hudson's injury was diagnosed as "concussion of the spine," a condition which gradually developed into paralysis. Within a few weeks, Hudson could not move his legs at all; in fact, he could not even sit. The doctor's orders were for him to stay in bed and rest. Still his condition worsened. At last he could only turn from side to side in the bed, and even that took great effort. He could not even hold a pen to write his own letters. He faced the possibility of never walking again.

In circumstances which would have dismayed and discouraged most other people, Hudson Taylor kept his thoughts fixed on the work in China. "Jennie, I need a map," he said one day.

She looked at him in surprise. "A map?"

"Yes, a map of China. I want to be able to see it from the bed. Our work is not finished."

Jennie smiled to herself as she fastened the map to the wall. She should have known that Hudson would persist no matter what the obstacles were. Patiently, she wrote the letters he dictated and read to him from the Bible. Daily they prayed together for missionaries to go to China.

There were still nine provinces in China with no missionaries. The China Inland Mission was extremely low in funds, and the flow of people asking about the work had trickled off. Hudson and Jennie had been praying for over two years for missionaries to these last nine provinces. He could not hold a pen, but Hudson could still speak the sentences which God put in his heart. Early in 1875, a pamphlet, *Appeal for Prayer on Behalf of More than a Hundred and Fifty Millions of Chinese,* was published. In this short book, Hudson did not directly ask people to be missionaries. Rather, he simply asked them to join him in praying for eighteen missionaries to form nine teams to reach the inland provinces of China.

The response was overwhelming! Jennie brought in stacks of letters every day.

"Hudson, we must have help," she insisted. "We cannot keep up with the mail on our own."

Hudson nodded his agreement. "You are right, of course. We need people to help answer letters and arrange interviews."

Although Hudson was still confined to bed, he worked at a furious pace. Every moment of the day was taken up with responding to letters with the help of volunteers, with prayer meetings, with council meetings, with interviews with potential missionaries.

It was not long before the eighteen missionaries Hudson had prayed for sailed for China. And still the flow of letters continued. More than sixty people volunteered to go to China, and the money needed by the China Inland Mission came to Hudson and Jennie in strange and miraculous ways.

Ten years had passed since that day on the beach at

Brighton when the China Inland Mission was born. They were years full of personal tragedy and spiritual challenge. And now Hudson Taylor, though lying flat on his back and in pain, gave glory to God for the spread of the gospel across China.

CHAPTER 10

The China Inland Mission was not the only subject of prayer among those who gathered around Hudson Taylor's bedside. One after the other, friends came to call and assure him they were praying for his recovery. Hudson himself seemed unconcerned about his own health: God had accomplished great things for the Mission even though its leader lay helpless. The prayers of those who loved Hudson were answered, and he returned to full health and was able to go once more to China.

After years of unfailing prayer and determined effort, the China Inland Mission now stood on the threshold of great opportunity—one which no other missionary organization had ever faced. So far, the missionaries in each province were traveling missionaries, and now the Mission had the opportunity to establish permanent mission stations in many of the provinces. The money needed to accomplish this was not coming in at a very fast rate, but Hudson never stopped believing that God would provide for His workers.

"We must go on," he would say to Jennie or to anyone who would listen. "We have always acted on faith, and we must not turn back now. God has opened too many doors to let us be stopped simply because of money."

Walking in the hills of Wuchang in 1882, Hudson pondered the problem. He counted in his head the number of workers needed to meet the most pressing needs. He pictured place after place and thought of the millions of Chinese still to be reached. "Seventy," he said aloud, though he was alone. "The Lord sent the seventy out, two by two, and we shall do this, also."

Hudson hurried back to share this idea, which he believed the Lord had put into his mind, with his coworkers. At first, some of them thought this was impossible. "Even if we could find that many people willing to come," one said, "how would we raise the money we need for all those missionaries?"

"God will provide the workers and the money," Hudson insisted. Anyone looking at him could see that he believed sincerely what he was saying. "It is God Who will send the people, and He will know what they need."

The group held several prayer meetings and started discussing Hudson's contagious idea. Gradually, Hudson's sense of excitement caught on. It would take a lot of faith to ask God for that many people and that much money. They asked themselves, "Do we have the faith to believe God will do it?" Eventually they decided it would be realistic to plan to expand the missionary work over a period of three years.

"If only we could meet again and have a united praise meeting when the last of the seventy has reached China," suggested one missionary.

"We shall be widely scattered then," said another. "Why not have the praise meeting now? Why not give thanks for the seventy now?"

And so the band of missionaries held a meeting thanking God for the seventy new workers before even one of them had arrived on Chinese soil.

Although the Mission was not without problems, the work continued to expand. In 1886, Hudson suggested that the Mission plan to accept one hundred new missionaries in 1887—in one year! Again, some raised the objection of the cost, and again Hudson responded by repeating how urgent the need was to reach the millions of Chinese people who still had not heard the name of Christ.

The energetic leader of the Mission set out on yet another voyage to England to help find the workers needed for China. He made three visits to nearby Ireland and four to Scotland, speaking on the subject of evangelizing the world. He also spoke at more than twenty conferences and retreats in England. Everywhere he went, he asked people to pray for the hundred to come forward.

And they did come forward. They came from all corners of England, Ireland, and Scotland. More than six hundred people offered themselves as candidates, and Hudson was overwhelmed with requests for interviews. He and his committee were careful to select only those who were completely dedicated to serving the Lord and who fully understood the harshness of life in China.

At the same time, others prayed and worked for the funds needed to send these volunteers on this voyage which would change their lives. Miraculously, the money was raised. In

November of 1887, Hudson Taylor stood before the friends of the Mission and announced that God had given the hundred for which they had been praying—and that all the money they needed was available for all of them to go.

Because of one man's simple and constant obedience, the China Inland Mission was now a major missionary force in China.

CHAPTER 11

First, Hudson Taylor had prayed for twenty-four workers.

Then he heard the Lord telling him to find the seventy.

And then, though it seemed impossible, he was challenged to find the hundred.

And now the thousand began to come forward and offer themselves to the mission work in China.

After traveling throughout England, Scotland, and Ireland, Hudson Taylor was anxious to return to China. He had already made six trips to that vast country, and though he was no longer a young man, he wanted to go again. Hudson knew he had to return to England from time to time to find workers and raise the money needed for them to go to China, and of course he always enjoyed the opportunity to visit with friends and family. His children were grown, and it gave him great satisfaction that one of his sons was a missionary to China. He was very pleased with the growth of the Mission, which had already gone unbelievably far beyond his early dreams.

But in spite of this amazing progress, Hudson missed being among the Chinese people personally. While others began to see him as a great leader, Hudson continued to think of himself as a simple, humble missionary wanting only to obey God.

Hudson and Jennie continued to work together in many ways at the Mission headquarters. Their years together, working side by side, had been very productive. Dozens of letters arrived each day from people interested in knowing more about the China Inland Mission, and dozens of invitations arrived with requests for Hudson Taylor to speak to large groups of people.

Jennie sat looking through the towering stacks of mail, as she did most mornings. With two particular letters in her hand she turned to her husband, who was bent over his own work.

"Hudson, what about these letters inviting you to visit North America?" she asked. "Should you consider going? Mr. Moody and Mr. Erdman are so determined; they feel they simply must have you speak at their conventions this summer."

Hudson sighed. "They are very kind to invite me, but I have had no assurance from the Lord that the work should be extended by traveling to America. And I am anxious to return to China."

"Perhaps you should reconsider." Jennie turned back to her work without saying anything more. There was no need to pressure her husband. Hudson would listen to God's voice and do just exactly what he should do.

Although he had already turned down an invitation to visit America, Hudson could not keep ignoring the persistent letters. He thought and prayed some more.

"Jennie," he said a few days later, "I will go to America, after all. I believe now that the Lord has a special reason for the repeated invitations I have received."

Jennie simply smiled and agreed.

In the end, Hudson made plans to visit America and speak at several meetings on his way back to China in the summer of 1888. To his delight, his son and daughter-in-law decided to travel with him. Before he left on this important voyage, he stood before the yearly meeting of the China Inland Mission in London. His message had a simple point: "God is moving; are we also moving? Are we ready to go with Him?"

Hudson's challenging words rang in his own ears during the weeks he spent in the United States and Canada. He spoke at meetings of hundreds of students and presented the enormous spiritual needs of the huge nation of China. Hudson was overwhelmed by the response he received—unexpected gifts of money and dozens of volunteers to go to China. To his utter amazement, when Hudson left for China in October of 1888, fourteen others sailed with him. Once again, he marveled at the guidance God had given. If he had once again turned down the invitations to speak in America, he would never have known of the love and eagerness of the American people to help in the work of the China Inland Mission.

After a brief stay in China, Hudson Taylor again visited North America and helped to organize a branch of the China Inland Mission there. Then he traveled on to Sweden and Norway, speaking to as many as five thousand people at one time. Everywhere he went, people were keenly interested in hearing about China. Even the queen of Sweden invited Hudson Taylor for a private audience!

Two things were clear to Hudson Taylor now. First, he should be looking not for seventy or one hundred workers, but one thousand new volunteers for China. Second, these workers would not just come from England but from countries all over the world. Because he strongly believed these two things, Hudson was now more eager to accept invitations to speak and to travel to the far corners of the earth if that was necessary to find one thousand new workers.

The first trip to America, which he had not been eager to make, had dramatically changed the role Hudson Taylor played with the China Inland Mission. During the next fifteen years, he spent less and less time in China and more and more time finding the workers God was sending to carry on the work. He continued visiting the United States, Canada, Sweden, Norway, France, Germany, Switzerland, Australia, and New Zealand.

Just as in the early days God had given Hudson Taylor a vision for working in the heart of China, now God had given him a vision for including Christians all around the world in telling the good news of Jesus Christ to the Chinese people.

CHAPTER 12

As the ship glided into the harbor at Shanghai in April of 1905, Hudson Taylor gazed upon the landmarks which had become so familiar over the last fifty years. On his first trip to Shanghai, Hudson had been a young man full of vision and ideals. But he had not known what to expect from living in China. At the age of twenty-one, his heart had burned passionately to tell the good news of God's love to the Chinese people. He never imagined that his humble work would someday lead to a worldwide organization to send missionaries to China.

Hudson made his way into the city and arrived at the Mission's Shanghai headquarters. Even before he reached his room, he smelled the lovely fragrance of the flowers that filled it. He looked around at the many flower arrangements which welcomed him, and he began to read the cards attached. *How kind they all are to share my grief,* he thought to himself.

Hudson had spent the winter in Switzerland mourning the loss of Jennie. She had seemed quite well when the summer began, but later had had to spend several weeks in bed. Faithfully and lovingly, Hudson had sat at Jennie's bedside until at last it was obvious she would not recover. It was difficult for her to breathe, and Hudson was in anguish because he could do nothing to help her.

"Ask Him to take me quickly," she had whispered.

And Hudson had prayed. He had never had a harder prayer to pray, but for her sake, he cried out to God to free her. Within five minutes, Jennie was gone.

Hudson had stayed in Switzerland through the winter, but when spring came his heart turned again to China. He was no longer general director of the China Inland Mission, but he felt he could still be a good missionary. China had captured his heart as a boy and had never released its hold.

He was seventy-three years old now, and he knew that traveling in China could be difficult. But he was determined to go. His son, Howard, a medical doctor, and his wife had traveled with Hudson before, and they agreed once more to go with him to China.

And so he returned to Shanghai, and from there traveled to the other places which held special meaning for him. Free of the task of overseeing the mission, he could instead visit mission stations far away from Shanghai; he could once again travel to the inland provinces of this country he loved.

At Yang-chou he took the easy path to the cemetery where Maria and four of their children were buried. It was Easter and, rather than feeling sorrowful, Hudson's heart was filled with sweet memories: Maria as the gentle young woman he had fallen in love with; Gracie's high voice chattering eagerly; the boys who chased each other and squealed through the house; the tiny baby who had made Maria happy during her last weeks. He had long ago stopped grieving, and now he knew that he would soon be reunited with these members of his family.

Next, Hudson and his son and daughter-in-law took a steamship to Hankow, a busy center for the Mission, which was connected to villages lying deep in the heart of China. Hudson visited happily with old friends who had worked in China for half a century.

"Hudson, you have become such a traveler," said one old friend. "But we certainly did not expect you to visit way out here."

"My friend," Hudson replied, "I intend to go on from here. I can never see enough of inland China to satisfy me."

"But you are an old man," his friend teased.

"No older than you," Hudson replied. "You're still here."

The expression on his friend's face grew serious. "I could never leave the work. I could never stay away from China."

"Then you know how I feel," Hudson said, and the two friends stood together sharing a silence which said they understood each other.

In the fifty years since Hudson Taylor's first journey to China, many improvements had taken place which made traveling a great deal easier than it had been. The journey from Hankow north to Hunan had once taken two weeks of strenuous, tedious travel. Now the trip was made comfortably in six hours on the sleek, efficient railroad. In the past, visiting five different mission stations around Hunan would have been a major project; now even an old man could travel easily from village to village encouraging generations of Christians.

But even modern travel could not make Hudson Taylor a

young man again. More and more often, he was too tired for evening meetings, or even to have supper with his son and daughter-in-law.

"There, Father," Howard said, patting his father's pillow, "that should make you more comfortable. Lie back and rest, and I will get your supper."

Hudson nodded at Howard and smiled at his daughter-in-law, who sat nearby looking at letters from England and a missionary newsletter.

"Aren't these pictures wonderful?" she asked. "I know traveling around makes it hard to keep up with your mail. Perhaps when you feel more rested—"

She stopped in the middle of her sentence when she heard Hudson gasp. She thought maybe he was going to sneeze, but instead he gasped again. The blank look on his face frightened her.

"Howard!" She ran to the door calling for her husband. "Howard, hurry!"

The end had come.

Howard rushed back into the room just in time to see his father take his last breath. In only a few seconds, the weight of seventy-three years in an earthly body passed away; the weary lines in Hudson's face disappeared. He looked like a child quietly sleeping in a peaceful room.

It was not a death that Howard and his wife witnessed. Rather, it was a swift and joyful entry into eternal life. Hudson Taylor bravely ventured on another journey in response to the voice of God.

DAVID LIVINGSTONE

MISSIONARY AND EXPLORER

by Dan Larsen

CHAPTER 1

The lion was about thirty yards away. It was as still as the flat rock it sat on. The hunter crouched behind a scraggly patch of bushes. Both barrels of his elephant gun were already cocked. This was closer than he had ever hoped to come to a lion in the wilds. But he had no choice now: This lion must die.

They had come out that morning, the great traveler and his native friends, the Bakhatla, to hunt the lions. For many days now, the lions had closed in on Mabotsa, the tiny village in the valley. They had come down from the hills, lean and hungry, to take easy prey among the villagers' herds of cattle and sheep. Night and day, their roars boomed off the hills, echoing throughout the valley. In the first attack, one lion charged among the sheep, killing nine while the herd stood still, too terrified to move.

The Bakhatla, "the People of the Monkey," were as terrified as their sheep. "We are bewitched!" they would cry. "Who ever saw the lion, the lord of the night, kill our cattle by day?" The lion was a creature of the night, the Bakhatla knew. But these lions came boldly near the village in the heat of day, killing almost lazily, feeding on only some of the carcasses, while leaving others to bloat in the sun.

"They must be stopped," the great traveler David Livingstone had said. The way to stop them, he knew, was to kill one and leave it lying in the field. The other lions would leave the area when they saw the dead one.

Today was the day of the hunt. David carried his heavy-caliber double-barreled rifle. The native schoolmaster of the village, a man named Mebalwe, also had a gun. The other natives carried spears. The lions were on a small hill covered with trees. The Bakhatla encircled the hill and slowly closed in, beating the tall weeds with their spears and chanting to drive the lions to the waiting guns of Livingstone and Mebalwe. But, one by one, the lions broke through the ring of spearmen and disappeared into the fields. The Bakhatla were too frozen with fear to throw their spears. Soon they had covered the hill. The lions were gone.

All but one. It was huge, the biggest lion that Mebalwe had ever seen. He stiffened and then touched David on the shoulder and pointed. Now David could see the lion, barely. Its tawny hide was the same color as the parched ground.

This is the one, David thought. But he had to get closer. *Lord, give me courage,* he prayed silently. Then he cocked both barrels of his gun and crept forward. The natives must not see that he was too afraid to act, he knew. He must show them the way of courage. But he was afraid. Very afraid.

The lion was not looking at him. Slowly he stalked, hoping to come to a spare patch of bushes about thirty yards from the lion. His palms were sweaty now, his mouth dry. Step by step, he closed in. There was the bush, just ahead.

Then the lion turned and looked at him. David froze. And

instantly he realized two things. One, the lion had known he was there, had known all along that he was coming. He saw this now in the lion's yellow eyes as they stared into his own. And, two, the bush was no better than a cobweb between him and the lion. The glare from the lion's eyes seemed to burn a path straight through the flimsy branches.

No time to wait now. Shaking, David raised his rifle and squeezed both triggers. As if punched by a giant fist, the lion was punched backward off the rock.

David's knees were shaking. He couldn't see the lion behind the rock. But he had seen it go down. One of the Bakhatla now shouted, "He is shot! He is shot!" David took a deep breath. Then he began reloading his rifle.

Just as he was tamping a lead ball into a barrel, he thought he glimpsed, out of the corner of one eye, a lion's tail from behind the flat rock. The tail was stiff, pointing straight up. That's what a lion did with its tail, he knew, just before. . .

"The lion! The lion!" came the screams. David looked up. All he saw was a tan blur, all he heard was the snapping of the dry branches of the bushes, and all he felt was a sudden horrible pain in his left shoulder.

He realized he was on the ground several yards from where his rifle lay, the lion on top of him, its teeth in his shoulder. Those pale eyes were huge now, only inches from his face. They were as icy and full of death as a snake's. The lion's breath was like rotten meat.

David felt himself being shaken, like a rat in a dog's mouth.

When the shaking stopped, the pain was gone. He felt nothing. His vision was blurred, and a sense of dreaminess, of floating, had come over him.

He didn't hear the rifle shots nor did he feel the lion let go of him. He didn't see it charge Mebalwe and clamp its teeth in his leg. Unknown to him, the bullets from his own gun, which had opened the lion's chest like an explosion, now finished their work, bleeding the last of the fierce life out of the beast. Finally, the lion dropped in the dust and lay still.

His shoulder would never be the same. In time it would heal some, but his left arm would hang stiff for years. The bone was crunched into splinters. Eleven tooth marks left their scars.

But tonight in the village of Mabotsa, which means, "A Marriage Feast," the Bakhatla held a celebration. Their white friend, their protector, had saved them. They would love him always, they swore. The feasting, laughing, and the stories of the day's hunt went on and on. But David Livingstone lay on soft grasses in a hut, tossing in fever, while a couple of the Bakhatla sponged him with cool water and prayed to his great God for his life.

Outside the village, the night was silent. There would be no roaring of the lions tonight. They would not come back, not to this place.

David Livingstone had come to Mabotsa from the south. He had traveled hundreds of miles, through plains, across rivers, and over mountains. His way led north, always to the north. His life's work waited for him in the north, he knew. "There is a vast plain to the north," Robert Moffat, the great missionary to Africa, had told him. "I have sometimes seen, in the morning sun, the smoke of a thousand villages where no missionary has ever been."

Where no missionary has ever been! When David heard these words, he knew what lay ahead of him in life. He just knew. "I will go at once to Africa," he had said to Moffat.

Until he met Moffat, David hadn't known he would go to Africa. But he had long known he would be a missionary. He had heard the call as a boy.

He was born on March 19, 1813, in the village of Blantyre in Lanarkshire, Scotland. His father was a poor tea merchant. When David was ten, he went to work in the Blantyre cotton mill. There he worked from six in the morning until eight in the evening. His job was to watch a cotton spinning frame and tie any threads of cotton that broke.

But though his body kept to the task, his mind was elsewhere. David had always wanted to learn new things. With half his first week's wages, he bought a Latin grammar book. This he propped up at work by his spinner so he could read a sentence here and there while he watched the cotton threads. Soon he also began to be tutored nights after work. Even after he left his teacher for the night, he would often stay up past midnight reading. His mother would have to take his books away and blow out his lamp.

His father, Neil Livingstone, was pleased to see that David, too, had a love of books and learning. He gave David history and travel books, classical works, and, most important to Neil Livingstone, the Bible.

But David's life was not all work and study. On weekends and holidays, he would tramp for miles and miles all over the countryside. He grew strong and developed great stamina. He couldn't know it then, but all this was preparing him for his life's work.

At eighteen, he was promoted to the position of spinner at the mill, a job that paid much better wages. David decided to save his money for the university. It would take many years, but David was determined to study to become a doctor and a missionary.

David had read of a doctor missionary in China. Perhaps he, too, could go to China and be like that man. Like the Great Physician, Jesus Christ, Who came to give life to all people, David longed to save lives in China.

He was accepted at the university in Glasgow, Scotland. One winter morning, he and his father began the long walk on the snowy road to Glasgow.

While at the university, David wrote a letter to the London Missionary Society, offering himself as a missionary to China. The directors of the society told him they would accept him if he went through a training course at a school in the little town of Chipping Ongar in Essex, near London, England.

At Ongar he met the man who would give him his life's vision. A tall, powerful man with a great bushy beard, Robert Moffat had just returned from Africa with stories of that huge, mysterious continent. Moffat told David of the "vast plain to the north" and the "smoke of a thousand villages where no missionary has ever been."

David knew he must go! He told the directors of the missionary society that he wished to go to Africa. They agreed to send him. "Go to the north," they had said, "to that plain of a thousand villages where no missionary has yet been."

On the morning of November 17, 1840, twenty-seven-year-old David Livingstone hugged his father on the Broom-ielaw quay in Glasgow before walking up the gangway to his waiting ship, the *George*. They held each other a long time. Unable to speak out loud the words they felt, they said good-bye. They would never see each other again.

The ship *George* sailed around the Cape of Good Hope and into the Bay of Algoa, where the Atlantic and Indian Oceans meet. Here David landed and began the long journey inland.

They went on horseback and on foot, with an oxcart for

their supplies. David's wanderings as a boy served him well now. He walked on and on tirelessly. Even the hardy African natives had trouble keeping up with him.

Isaac Taylor, a friend of David's at Chipping Ongar, would many years later describe his walk: "I remember his step, the characteristic forward tread, firm, simple, resolute, neither fast nor slow, no hurry and no dawdle, but which evidently meant getting there." Another friend would write, "Fire, water, stone wall would not stop Livingstone."

Nothing would stop him now. The north, on to the north. On to the smoke of a thousand villages.

The days were blistering hot, the nights clear and cold. They slept under the stars and huddled in blankets around the oxcart in the early morning, warming fingers on tin cups of steaming black coffee. During the hottest time of the day, they would stop to rest, sitting in the shade of the wagon.

They came to the village of Kuruman, where Robert Moffat had lived. Moffat was now home in England on a visit. Kuruman had once been a dry, barren place, but now it was filled with fruit trees, vines, and gardens. Moffat had been a gardener before he became a missionary, and he had used his skills here.

He had dug ditches to bring water from the hillsides two miles away. Then he'd planted trees and gardens, using the water to irrigate. Kuruman was now a place of beauty and rest.

But David was not here to rest: He stayed only long

enough to let the oxen recover. From Kuruman they went north to Lepelole. The people here called themselves the Bakwena, the "People of the Crocodile." David stayed here, waiting for word from the missionary society in London. Would they tell him to go on now, or wait here? Was this as far as he would go?

He waited for six months. No one who spoke English was with him now. He wanted to learn the language and habits of these people.

The Bakwena men went out daily to hunt. The women and children stayed in the village, the women working, the children playing. They all spent their days in fear, though, of the village witch doctor. This doctor said he could "smell" witchcraft. He could tell, he said, if a person committed a crime. At his word, that person would be put to death.

David knew he had to free these people from their fear of witchcraft. He knew the only way to do this was to teach them about the one true God. So as he learned their language, he began to tell them about God. "There is only one God," he had said to them, "one Father, Who wants the People of the Crocodile to be brothers, not enemies."

But David did not just talk. While in the village, he noticed how dry the ground was. The witch doctor was said to be a rainmaker, too. But despite his dances, charms, and prayers, no rain came. David said he would bring rain. With the only shovel in the village—one without a handle—he began to dig a canal from a nearby stream. Day by day, the men from the village began to dig with him, using stones, knives, and even their hands. Soon there was a canal with many smaller ditches running from it into the gardens. Droopy vegetables lifted their heads and grew; grass began to sprout; flowers appeared.

The witch doctor laughed to see that this clever white traveler had done what all his gods could not. The Bakwena began to believe it possible to be brothers, after all. This great white traveler, who worked with his hands as well as his heart, must indeed serve a great God!

In the village of the Bakwena, David started to build a house. But then the letter came. The missionary society said yes, go on to the north. Go beyond the places that other missionaries have gone to before. Go to the land of the smoke from a thousand villages.

And this was the journey that took David to the People of the Monkey in the village of Mabotsa—and to the lion.

His journey would not end here. It had hardly begun. Yet before he could go on, he needed time to rest and to heal and to build a school.

CHAPTER 3

The school had no desks, no chairs, and no pictures on the walls. The floor was the earth, the walls were mud brick, and the teacher was the great white traveler with the crippled left arm.

David Livingstone had now been in Africa for four years. He stayed here in the village of Mabotsa. The villagers helped him build a stone-and-brick house, and they asked him to live with and be one of them and teach their children.

At first the children were afraid of the white man who had killed the lion. He had a powerful God, they knew, a God Who gave him strength and protected him. He seemed to fear nothing. Why did he want the children to come to him in the schoolhouse? What would he do to them? They would not have come, but the Bakhatla chief and the schoolmaster, Mebalwe, said they must.

On the first day of school, the children discovered that they had nothing to fear. The white schoolmaster was as gentle and kind as he was strong and brave. He sat on the ground with the children and spoke their language and learned their games. Sometimes he would cry as he told them of his great God. This God was everyone's God, the white teacher said, a God Who loved the world so much that He came to earth to live as a man and to die as a man, so that anyone who believes in Him might live with Him forever.

David's days were very busy. He cut trees and made planks, built houses, gardened, taught in the school, doctored the sick and injured, and repaired guns and wagons and furniture and just about everything else. All the Bakhatla were his friends.

But David was lonely. He had no one to go home to at night, no one with whom to share his dreams and hopes and deepest thoughts.

One day he received glad news. His friend Robert Moffat was returning from England to the village of Kuruman. David set out on horseback to meet him. When he reached Kuruman, Moffat was not there yet. So after a day's rest, David rode south to meet him. He went 150 miles before he saw Moffat's wagon coming up the road.

From a distance, David waved to his friend. As he came nearer, he recognized Mrs. Moffat on the wagon bench. But sitting between Mr. and Mrs. Moffat was someone David did not recognize—a young woman in a sunbonnet. David and Moffat shook hands in the road. He bowed to Mrs. Moffat, then to the young woman next to her.

"David, this is my eldest daughter, Mary," Robert said.

David mumbled hello. She smiled and then looked down at her hands in her lap.

"It has been a long time, my friend," said Moffat, his hand on David's shoulder. "How are things in. . .David? David?"

David and Mary were soon engaged. David knew he had found the answer to his loneliness. It seemed perfect. The school in Mabotsa needed someone to teach the girls. Mary Moffat had been born in Africa and had spent many years there with her father. She knew the duties and hardships of missionary life. From the moment she saw him, she loved David Livingstone.

Before they could be married, though, there was much to do. David would have to return alone to Mabotsa to build a house for them. Meanwhile, he wrote to Colesberg, Africa, to get their marriage license, and he wrote to the mission directors in London, announcing his engagement and asking their approval for his plans for Mabotsa. He wanted to make the village a training center for missionaries, from which students would be sent out into surrounding areas. This was what Moffat had done in Kuruman.

On August 1, 1844, during his journey north to Mabotsa, David wrote a letter to Mary.

"Whatever friendship we feel toward each other," David wrote, "let us always look to Jesus as our common Friend and Guide, and may He shield you with His everlasting arms from every evil."

In Mabotsa David began building their house. Work left little time for him to think of Mary, who was waiting for him in Kuruman. But whenever he could, he would write to her. He sent this letter on September 12, 1844:

I must tell you of the progress I have made. . . . The walls are nearly finished, although the dimensions are fifty-two feet by twenty outside, or about the same size as the house in which you now reside. I began with stone, but when it was breast-high, I was obliged to desist from my purpose to build it entirely of that material. . . . A stone falling. . .caught by me in its fall by the left hand, and it nearly broke my arm over again. It swelled up again, and I fevered so much I was glad of a fire, although the weather was quite warm. I expected bursting and discharge, but Baba bound it up nicely, and a few days' rest put all to rights. . .six days have brought the walls up a little more than six feet.

The walls will be finished long before you receive this, and I suppose the roof, too, but I have still the wood of the roof to seek. It is not, however, far off. . . .

You must excuse soiled paper: My hands won't wash clean after dabbling mud all day. And although the above does not contain evidence of it, you are as dear to me as ever, and will be as long as our lives are spared. I am still your most affectionate

D. Livingstone

David also wrote Mary something of life in Mabotsa. In October 1844 he wrote:

*All goes on pretty well here; the school is sometimes
well, sometimes ill attended. I had a great objection
to school-keeping, but I find in that as in almost
everything else I set myself to as a matter of duty, I
soon become enamored of it. A boy came three times
last week, and on the third time could act as monitor
to the rest through a great portion of the alphabet.
He is a real Bakhatla, but I have lost sight of him
again. If I get them on a little, I shall translate some
of your infant-school hymns into Sichuana rhyme,
and you may yet, if you have time, teach the tunes to
them. I, poor mortal, am as mute as a fish in regard
to singing. . . .*

*And now I must again, my dear, dear Mary, bid
you good-bye. Accept my expressions as literally true
when I say, I am your most affectionate and still
confiding lover,*

D. Livingstone

The house was soon finished, the marriage licenses came from
Colesberg, and Mary came from Kuruman. Then in the village
of "A Marriage Feast," there was indeed a marriage feast.

CHAPTER 4

In Mabotsa the Bakhatla had all gathered in the little village road. They had not gathered today to celebrate, but to mourn, to say good-bye. The wagon was loaded, the oxen were harnessed, and the horses were saddled. The white traveler and his wife were ready.

Some of the Bakhatla came up to the Livingstones and said, "Do stay, please. We will build another house for you."

"We must go north," Livingstone had said. Not too long ago, another missionary had settled in Mabotsa, and David and Mary felt the time had come to move on. They, too, were sorry to leave their friends, the Bakhatla, but they wanted more than anything to be obedient to God and to go where He led them.

They came to the village of Chonuane, forty miles to the north. In Chonuane there lived the Bakwena, "the People of the Crocodile." The chief, Sechele, welcomed them with great kindness. Here Livingstone built another stone house for Mary and himself and a school. Here the Livingstones had their first child, a boy. They named him Robert, after Mary's father.

But they would not stay here long. Chonuane was a dry place: There were no streams or lakes, and one summer, month after month, there was no rain. The Livingstones would have to move on, David told the Bakwena. Then they would move with the Livingstones, the Bakwena told David.

And one morning everyone in the village, with all their possessions in carts and on their backs, started northward with David and Mary and little Robert.

They found a place to build another village by a river. They called this place Kolobeng. Here David, with the help of Chief Sechele, built another house for Mary and himself and yet another school. They dug ditches from the river into the villagers' gardens. The Livingstones were as busy as ever, David teaching the boys and preaching, building, fixing, and doctoring; Mary teaching the girls and taking care of baby Robert and their household.

They stayed here for several years. Mary had two more children, a boy, Thomas, and a girl, Agnes. They wondered how long this would be their home.

One day some messengers came to the village. They were from Chief Lechulatebe, they said, who lived by a great lake that lay hundreds of miles to the north on the other side of the Kalahari Desert. Lechulatebe had heard somehow of David Livingstone, the messengers said. Would the great traveler come north with them to see their chief?

David had heard of a lake across the Kalahari. Was this his destiny, the land of the smoke of a thousand villages? Now he would find out.

The river at Kolobeng was getting low. The rain had not come for months. Some of the Bakwena were grumbling that David's God could not bring rain. David wished to find a place with plenty of water. Perhaps these messengers from

Chief Lechulatebe brought the answer to this wish.

With three other travelers, Mr. Murray, Mr. Oswell, the hunter, and Colonel Steel, David set out with the messengers. They went over wooded hills and down into the bed of a wide river, long dry. They followed the riverbed northward. The country here was flat with thorny trees. Antelope grazed in the grasses. Monkeys climbed in the trees. At night, lions roared in the darkness.

But as they went, the ground became more and more sandy. The oxen went slower and slower as the wagon wheels sank deeper and deeper. The sun was scorching in the deep blue sky; they found no water.

At last they reached Lake Ngami, the home of Chief Lechulatebe. David and his three friends were the first white men ever to see this lake. It was huge, stretching beyond their sight. Here David learned of a land farther to the north, "full of rivers—so many that no one can tell their number—and full of trees."

David decided he must return for Mary and their children. Together they would cross Lake Ngami to find this land of rivers.

When they went back, Kolobeng was drier than ever. Mary and the children had moved to a hut nearer the river, now only a muddy trickle. Livingstone was convinced they could not live here in the desert of the south. They must go north.

They went in a caravan of eighty cattle and twenty men on horseback. Mary and the children rode in one of the wagons.

They would eventually reach Lake Ngami, but not on this journey. This time they would get only so far as the Zouga River. As they rested there, many of the traveling party became ill. David and Mary's own children tossed in fever for days. Finally David decided to return south to the drier air of the desert. The air there, he knew, was healthier to breathe.

Their children recovered, and months later they set out again. This journey did take them to the lake. David and Mary stood on the shore and laughed as their three little children paddled and splashed in the cool water.

They would not go farther north to find the land of many rivers, not this time. The Livingstone children again became ill. They had to go back.

They tried again almost two years after David's first journey to Lake Ngami. But this time there was no water. Even the underground streams, which the natives knew how to find, were dried up. An accident with the wagon carrying their water barrels cost them all the water they had brought. For four days they went without water.

Of all the caravan, David suffered the worst. His agony was in hearing the parched little voices of his children as they cried for water. He suffered even more as he saw the pain and fear in his wife's eyes. He knew she was struggling to be brave and cheerful. When he looked into her eyes, he saw not blame or bitterness, only love. He would later write of this time:

The next morning, the less there was of water the more thirsty the little rogues became. The idea of

*their perishing before our eyes was terrible. It would
almost have been a relief to me to have been re-
proached with being the entire cause of the catastro-
phe, but not one syllable of upbraiding was uttered
by their mother, though the tearful eye told the agony
within. In the afternoon of the fifth day, to our inex-
pressible relief, some of the men returned with a supply of that fluid of which we had never before felt the
true value.*

At last they reached the lake! Now David could look into
his wife's eyes and see only relief, not dread.

On the shore of the lake, David met another chief from farther north. This chief's name was Sebituane. He was a powerful chief with a large tribe. In his travels, David had heard of
this chief, and he eagerly accepted Sebituane's invitation to
come north with him to his village in the land of the lakes.

They traveled eastward around Lake Ngami. Farther north,
they came to a wide river. David discovered that this river, the
Zambezi, which flowed into the Indian Ocean, could be a way
into central Africa from the coast. No one had ever visited this
part of the African continent.

As they rode the gentle waves in canoes, David saw a vision. Missionaries and traders could come in from the east or
west coast. The missionaries could build schools in the villages
and teach these people about Jesus Christ, Who died for them.
They could teach the people new trades and skills. Some of the
villages were so poor that children starved to death.

As they continued northward, David learned of another reason to open up a way into central Africa: slavery. Sometimes slave traders bought children from poor natives; sometimes villages were raided. Old people were murdered; huts were burned, and children were snatched away from their families and herded to the coast in chains. Many died of starvation, and some died of heartache on the journey.

David burned inside at the thought of slavery. He would find a way to open up central Africa, build missionary training centers and schools, and unite the peoples against the slave trade. A way to the coast would allow these people to trade their ivory, coffee, and cotton—and not their children.

Much exploration of this area would be needed. But that would have to wait. David's children became sick again and again as they traveled through this humid, swampy area. The air was healthier in the desert to the south, but there was no water there. With his heart breaking, he realized there was only one answer: Mary and the children must return to England while he and his three friends explored farther to the north, to find an area where they could build a home. It had to be a high, dry land with a good supply of water—a lake or a large river. When he was finished with their house, David would send for his family. There they would build a missionary training center. There he and Mary could raise their family. Their travels would be over.

But now a very long journey lay ahead of them. They turned south once again, this time to go all the way back to Cape Town on the southern coast. There they would say good-bye—for awhile.

CHAPTER 5

Livingstone guessed he would need two years. That would be enough time to find a good spot and build their home. It would be the longest two years of his life! (He didn't know that it would turn out to be almost five.) Before he left Cape Town, he wrote a letter to his wife.

My dearest Mary,
How I miss you now and the dear children! . . . I see no face now to be compared with the sunburnt one which has so often greeted me with its kind looks. . . . Take the children all around you and kiss them for me. Tell them I have left them for the love of Jesus, and they must love Him, too, and avoid sin, for that displeases Jesus. I shall be delighted to hear of you all safe in England. . . .

David also wrote to his daughter, Agnes, who was then four years old.

My Dear Agnes,
This is your own little letter. Mamma will read it to you and you will hear her just as if I were speaking to you. . . .

*I am still at Cape Town. You know you left me
there when you all went into the big ship and
sailed away. Well, I shall leave Cape Town soon.
Malatsi has gone for the oxen, and then I shall go
away back to Sebituane's country, and see Seipone
and Meriye, who gave you the beads and fed you
with milk and honey.*

*I shall not see you again for a long time, and I
am very sorry. I have given you back to Jesus, your
Friend—your Papa Who is in heaven.*

A few days later David climbed into the oxcart and started
on the long journey north.

He stopped at Kuruman to see the Moffats, and they gave
him discouraging news. A band of slave-trading Boers had
raided Chief Sechele's village of Kolobeng. They had shot
many of Sechele's people, the Bakwena, and had stolen all
their cattle. They had even broken into the house that David
and Mary had lived in and taken the furniture and torn up all
his books and destroyed his medicines.

Staying with the Moffats was Masebele, the wife of
Sechele. She had escaped the village with her baby. Sechele
had also escaped, she said, but they had not been together, and
she did not know where he went.

"I hid in a cleft in the rock, with this little baby," she said.
She sat rocking the baby, who was asleep. "The Boers came
closer and closer, shooting with their guns. They came 'til

they were on the rock just above my head. I could see the muzzles of the guns above the clefts as they fired. The baby began to scream, and I felt sure that they would hear us and capture us, but I took off these armlets and gave them to baby to play with. That kept baby quiet, and the Boers passed on without finding us."

"The Boers have made up their minds to close the country," David now wrote to his wife. "I am determined to open it. Time will show who will win. I will open a path through the country—or PERISH."

They went north again, across the great Kalahari Desert. By day they saw herds of antelope and buffalo. They saw the ostrich and the cheetah streaking through the dry grasses. By night they heard the lions pacing and snarling all around their camp.

They came to a wide river, too deep for the wagons. They paddled across the river on a raft to a wide, marshy grassland. Here the water was ankle deep and the grasses knee high. They had to leave the raft and wade.

The grass was rough and very sharp. It bit into the men's legs as they waded. David's pant were soon torn out at the knees. He cut his handkerchief in two and wrapped his knees with the pieces.

They soon came to deeper water. This was too deep to wade in. The grasses grew so thick here that they would have to cut their way. One of the men shouted and pointed. There was a path where the grasses had been trampled into the water, probably by a hippopotamus. "We could swim through here," the man had said.

"No, look!" another said. "There are snakes swimming in the water. Their bite is deadly."

They saw some trees in the distance, and when they arrived there a couple of the men climbed the trees to scout the land.

"Look, there is deeper water downriver!" one of the men shouted. "I think our raft can pass through there."

They let the raft float downstream to the deeper water and began to paddle through. The mosquitoes were thick in the hot, humid afternoon air. The men paddling had to stop often and swat at their sweaty arms and legs. At times the water was too shallow to paddle in, and the men would have to jump off the raft and push. Their shoulders and backs ached, and the sweat dripped off their noses and stung their eyes.

They came to thicker grasses again. But the water was too shallow for paddling, so they had to go on and on downstream, looking for a way through the grasses. The afternoon passed and evening came. They still had not found a way through.

As the sun was dropping under the horizon, the men saw a village on the north bank, behind them. They decided to paddle back across the river and see if they could stay there for the night.

They pulled the raft onto the bank and climbed up a low hill into the village. As they neared the first huts, Livingstone stopped suddenly and stared. Then he threw his head back and laughed. These were friends! He recognized them as some of Sebituane's people, the Makololo. He had met them on his last journey with his family.

Now cries of joy came from the darkening streets. "Livingstone! Our friend!"

A man came up to David and cried as the two of them embraced. Then the man stood back, laughing. "He has dropped among us from the clouds," he said, "yet came riding on the back of a hippopotamus. We Makololo thought no one could cross the Chobe River without our knowledge, but here he drops among us like a bird."

That night the missionaries sat under the stars with their Makololo friends, and they ate and talked and laughed. The next day, the travelers and many of the Makololo went back to the raft. The Makololo took the wagons apart and brought them, piece by piece, back to the village. They drove the oxen into the river, making them swim to the other side. The Makololo knew the ways though the grasses to the south bank. They took the wagons and the oxen to this bank, and there they put the wagons back together.

In a few days, the Makololo took David and his men to the capital of the Makololo, a village called Linyanti, where six thousand Makololo lived. Here, too, lived Sekeletu, the son of Sebituane, whom David had met on his last journey. David and Sebituane had become close friends in the few weeks they spent together, but sadly, Sebituane caught fever and died. Now Sekeletu ruled in his place. He was as kind as his father had been.

The two now met in the village street, and Sekeletu brought David to his hut. They gave each other gifts, and they talked of Sebituane and of the slave traders and of David's work in Sekeletu's country.

David and his men stayed here for a few weeks. Sekeletu quickly grew to love David. He began to call him "my new father." They sat together one morning by Sekeletu's fire, drinking coffee and talking. Sekeletu smiled. "Your coffee tastes better than that of the traders," he said, "because they like my ivory, but you like me."

At night David, standing on a wagon, read his Bible to the Makololo. In silence the people would shake their heads in wonder as they heard the stories of Jesus and His followers.

During their talks, David told Sekeletu of his desire to open a road from the coast into the center of the country. Up this road missionaries and doctors and teachers could come; down this road the African people could carry their ivory and cotton and coffee to the coast where they could sell them. This would open up the country, David said, and would do away with the slave trade.

"I like this vision," Sekeletu said. He was beaming. Later, he called a gathering of the village leaders and told them of David's plans.

Sekeletu wanted to send men with David to guide him in his quest. Some of the leaders said no. "Where is the white doctor taking you?" asked one old man. "He is throwing you away! Your garments already smell of blood!" But others said yes. They would not agree to help just anyone, they said. But this man had earned their respect and their love. He was not like the traders who came through the village, they said. He wanted nothing for himself. He wanted only to help these people and to stop the horrible slave trade. If he would serve them, then they would serve him and, yes, even die for him.

They came to David late that night, Sekeletu and three of his chiefs. Sekeletu was smiling. "Yes, my new father," he said, "we will help you. We will go with you wherever you wish to go."

CHAPTER 6

The cry went throughout the camp. "The Njambi are coming!"

Carrying swords and spears, faces streaked with war paint, the Njambi came. In the camp, the Makololo scattered about, grabbing their spears and rifles, yelling to one another, crying out to their gods for protection.

The great white traveler remained seated on his camp stool. He held his double-barreled rifle across his knees.

Off in the forest, the drums were growing louder and louder. A warrior stepped out from the trees into the camp, his face in a fierce scowl. "The chief must have a man, an ox, a gun, powder, some cloth, or a shell. If not, you must go back. Or die."

David shook his head. "Tell the chief—" Just then the chief stepped into the clearing. Behind him came several warriors carrying spears, all pointed at David on his stool. The warriors began nodding to one another and gesturing with their spears toward David. Behind David, the Makololo were crouched, aiming their rifles at the strange warriors, holding up their spears, ready to spring.

Now the chief barked, "You heard my payment. I must have a man, an ox, a gun, powder, cloth, or a shell, or you go back. Or die."

The men on both sides were murmuring now. The murmur

rose to a clamor.

"Be seated," David said. There was no fear in that voice. It was quiet and steady. Suddenly everyone was silent, tensed. *Would the strangers attack?* the Makololo wondered. *Would their chief strike down this white man?* the Njambi wondered.

The chief, his eyes fixed on David's face, slowly sat down. His warriors stared at one another.

"Why do you ask me to pay to walk on the ground of God, our common Father?" David asked calmly,

The chief did not answer. To this question he had no answer. All the peoples of Africa called all the land "common." They believed it was God's, not theirs.

But for some tribes, things had changed. The terrible slave trade—the raiding, destroying, and the murdering—had turned these peoples bitter. They were once friendly and trusting; now they were suspicious of everybody. They had become greedy. They demanded payment of anyone who wished to travel through their land. Especially they wanted "man," slaves. This, too, they had learned from the slave traders.

The chief of the Njambi ignored David's question. He threw his chin up. "You must give me man," he said. "Man or go back."

"Never," David said. "I will die before I give one of my brothers into slavery." He stood up and went into his tent. Then he came out carrying several bundles. He offered the chief a shirt. The chief said no. He added beads. The chief shook his head. He added a large handkerchief. The chief growled, then said again that he wanted man.

His warriors had again stirred themselves into a frenzy. One of them now whooped shrilly and charged at David, his sword raised.

David did not flinch. Just as the warrior came within reach, he whipped his rifle up and stuck the barrel on the man's chin.

The man shrieked and ran into the forest. Slowly, David lowered his rifle. His eyes were on the chief, still sitting on the ground. "We will not strike the first blow," David said. "If you do, the guilt of blood is on your head."

The chief's warriors all held their spears ready. The Makololo, too, were ready. The Njambi chief saw the look on David's face. He saw the spears and guns of the Makololo aimed at him and his men. Then he looked down at his hands. They relaxed their grip on the spear. He stood up and bowed slightly to David. "You may pass," he said quietly. Then he and his warriors disappeared into the forest.

Twenty-seven young Makololo men had gone with David. All of them set out for the Zambezi River to the north. David had decided to travel up the Zambezi until it turned to the east. They would then leave the Zambezi and strike westward on the Kassai River, then northwest across the Kwango River to the Lucala River. Then it would be due west on to Loanda on the coast.

At first things went well. But as they passed out of the lands of Chief Sekeletu, they began to have trouble with some of the tribes who were not friendly to travelers. They had not had to fight yet, but they had come close, as with the Njambi.

"Man, ox, gun, or tusk you must give me," each chief would say, or David and his men would not be able to pass through. "Man" David would never give; "ox" he could hardly spare; "gun" he had only enough of for themselves, for hunting; "tusk" he had, but he hated to part with these. They were from Sekeletu who sent them with David so he could begin trade for Sekeletu's people on reaching Loanda.

They had over fifteen hundred miles to go to reach the coast. They had to cross streams and pass through flat, scorched lands. At times they went through forests so thick that they had to chop down trees so the wagons could pass through. This was slow, painful work. David was almost constantly ill with the African fever now. It weakened him so much that he could barely hold himself up while riding his ox. The fever burned in him day after day, week after week. He grew thinner and thinner. Many times he was delirious and lay in his tent tossing and moaning, bathed in sweat.

His Makololo friends became worried for him. They had grown to love him on this journey. He had proved himself to be a true brother to them. They knew he would give his life for them, and they swore they would give theirs for him.

Then the rains came. Day after day, rain dripped from the leaves and the hanging vines onto their heads as they passed through forests, and it poured on them as they crossed grassy plains and streams. Even their canvas tents became soaked through. At night the rain would drip in their faces as they slept in their wet blankets. Their clothes became moldy and clung to their raw skin.

In some of the villages they passed through, the people whispered to the Makololo that David Livingstone was leading them to their deaths. Tired and homesick and soaked from the rains, the Makololo began to wonder. Was it true? Where were they going?

David saw the change in his friends. They were growing more silent and sullen, more disheartened. Would they abandon him? Could he even blame them if they did?

One night David sat huddled in a wet blanket around a sputtering, hissing fire with several of the Makololo. The rain dripped steadily from the tree branches overhead. The fire would soon be out, it seemed, and there was no more dry wood anywhere. Earlier that day, some of the men had come to him and threatened to return. "If you go back, still I shall go on," he had said. Now he left the fire and crawled into his wet tent and lay there shivering with fever. He had never felt so alone, so lost, so hopeless.

As he lay there, he thought of his dear Mary and their children. He wondered what their lives were like now in England, without him. As he wondered when he would see them again, his tears flowed down his weather-beaten cheeks.

The flap to his tent opened, and one of his closest Makololo friends, Mohorisi, crawled to him. He reached out and gently touched David's cheek.

"We will never leave you," Mohorisi said, his voice shaking.

Then there were two, three, four men in the tent. They, too, were sobbing gently. "We will die for you. We spoke in bitterness before. We will not leave you. You will see what we can do!"

CHAPTER 7

David and the Makololo came out onto a high plain and there below them was the sea, sparkling in the sun. The Makololo had never seen the sea. They stood now without moving or speaking, simply staring at the water.

"We marched along with our father," one of them would later say, "believing that what the ancients had always told us was true, that the world has no end; but all at once the world said to us, 'I am finished; there is no more of me!' "

The journey had taken over six months. David had suffered again and again from the African fever. Now walking into the streets of Loanda, he was bone thin.

They stayed here for several weeks. The Makololo got jobs unloading a coal ship. David became friends with the captain, a British man. "You have worked and traveled without rest for fourteen years," the captain said. "You are ill. Come home with us and rest—come see your wife and daughter and your sons again. All Britain will cheer to see you."

David wanted badly to go home. But he was responsible for twenty-seven young men who had come fifteen hundred miles with him and pledged their lives to him. He could not just leave them here. No, he told the captain, he would have to take the Makololo back. They were far from home and would never find their way back without him. David had learned navigation skills from a ship captain, and he used these to find his way across Africa. He must guide his men home.

But he did send his journal home. In all his travels, he had written of places, people, the land, the rivers, the mountains —and the slave trade. His information would later prove valuable to the world in understanding much of the land then called "the Dark Continent." His written accounts would do much to stop slavery in the world.

They started back to Linyanti. David had a new canvas tent as a gift from the British captain. The Makololo carried, bundled in their packs, new striped European suits and bright red caps, gifts from the sailors on the captain's ship. David carried everything he owned in four tin canisters, each about fifteen inches square. One held shirts, pants, and shoes; the second, medicines; the third, books; and the fourth, a lantern. Whenever they passed through villages, he would light this lantern at night, hang it from a wagon, and preach to the natives. They would stare fascinated at the lantern while David spoke of the light that came into the world. "The darkness is passing away," he would say, "and the real light is already shining: God is light, and there is no darkness in Him at all." And his listeners would wonder about this God Who called people to walk in light and not in darkness.

As David and his Makololo friends journeyed westward, they saw more and more darkness. In the villages where they rested, the slavers would sometimes lead captives through the

streets—captives from other tribes and other lands. Men, women, and children were herded like cattle, chained one to
another with forked poles on their necks and iron bands on
their wrists. David saw that many of the wristbands dangled
empty, and he knew why they were empty. In his journeys, he
would many times pass by the bodies of people who had died
as they walked in these chains and had been thrown to the
side of the path. Many had died of starvation or thirst, but
many more died for another reason.

"It is brokenheartedness of which the slaves die," David
would later write in his journal. "Even children, who showed
wonderful endurance in keeping up with the chained gangs,
would sometimes hear the sound of dancing and the merry tin-
kle of drums in passing near a village. Then the memory of
home and happy days proved too much for them. They cried
and sobbed, the broken heart came on, and they rapidly sank."

He had already determined to destroy the slave trade. A
few years earlier, while in Cape Town after seeing his family
off to England, he had written a letter to the mission directors
in London telling them of his hope.

*Consider the multitudes that in the providence of God
have been brought to light in the country of Sebituane;
the probability that in our efforts to evangelize we
shall put a stop to the slave trade in a large region,
and by means of the highway into the north which
we have discovered bring unknown nations into the*

sympathies of the Christian world. . . . Nothing but a strong conviction that the step will lead to the glory of Christ would make me orphanize my children. . . . Should you not feel yourselves justified in incurring the expense of their support in England, I shall feel called upon to renounce the hope of carrying the gospel into that country. . . . But stay, I am not sure; so powerfully convinced am I that it is the will of our Lord that I should go, I will go, no matter who opposes; but from you I expect nothing but encouragement.

From the directors he got nothing but encouragement.

The directors of the London Missionary Society signified their cordial approval of my project by leaving the matter entirely to my own discretion. And I have much pleasure in acknowledging my obligations to the gentlemen composing that body for always acting in an enlightened spirit, and with as much liberality as their constitution would allow.

The slave trade was but one darkness; witchcraft was another. The witch doctors killed as many of their own people as the slavers ever did. The witch doctors would make accused people drink poison to prove their innocence or guilt. If the person died, he was guilty, the witch doctors said. If he lived, he was innocent. The people in the villages lived in fear of their witch doctor. To disobey his law was death, they believed.

David told the people not to fear the witch doctors. The poison is what kills, he told them, not the witch doctors' magic. Do not walk in darkness, in fear, he told them, but believe in Jesus Christ, Who came to set people free from fear and darkness and death.

Despite the darkness in this land, David vowed to fight the darkness with the light.

They came into Libonta, the first village of Chief Sekeletu, as heroes. Everyone in the village came out into the streets to cheer David and his twenty-seven men. He had kept his word. He had safely brought the twenty-seven back to their home. They held a day of thanksgiving on July 23, 1855.

David wrote in his journal:

The men decked themselves out in their best, for all had managed to preserve their suits of European clothing, which, with their white and red caps, gave them a rather dashing appearance. They tried to walk like soldiers, and called themselves "my braves." Having been again saluted with salvos from the women, we met the whole population, and having given an address on divine things, I told them we had come that day to thank God before them all for His mercy in preserving us from dangers, from

*strange tribes and sicknesses. We had another ser-
vice in the afternoon. They gave us two fine oxen to
slaughter, and the women have supplied us abun-
dantly with milk and meal. This is all gratuitous,
and I feel ashamed that I can make no return. My
men explained the whole expenditure on the way
hither, and they remarked gratefully: "It does not
matter; you have opened a path for us, and we shall
have sleep." Strangers from a distance come flocking
to see me, and seldom come empty-handed. I distribute all presents among my men.*

They went on to Linyanti. Sekeletu welcomed David as
his own father. He was excited to hear that David had found
a way to the west coast.

"But it is a long, hard way," David said. And he now wondered if a better way was to travel along the Zambezi River to
the east coast.

"We shall try," Sekeletu said. This time Sekeletu would
send 120 men, along with oxen for riding and for food.

This time when they set out, Sekeletu himself went with
David. They traveled down the Chobe River to where it met
the Zambezi River. Some paddled canoes while others drove
the oxen along the bank.

Thunder was booming in the night sky as they came to a
thick forest. Just as they passed through the first trees, rain

came. David was on land with a small band of the Mako-lolo. The other had drifted downriver in the canoes. The tents and most of the blankets were in the canoes. The men in the forest had only a few blankets and supplies; they would have to sleep without a tent tonight. It was pitch dark among the trees now. Lightning raced across the sky in wide bands, and in these brief flashes the men picked their way deeper and deeper into the forest. They found a tall tree with thick foliage and lay down under it. They were soaked and shivering and aching.

David lay hugging his knees, his teeth chattering. Suddenly he felt a hand touch his shoulder. He looked up but could see no one. Then two strong hands draped a blanket over him, and Sekeletu's voice said, "Here, my father, is my blanket. You take it to keep you warm."

David tried to refuse, but Sekeletu tucked the blanket around his feet and back. "You must," Sekeletu said, and then he went off under another tree and lay down to sleep in the rain.

It was March 3, 1856. They had come into Tette, an inland Portuguese station on the Zambezi River. They were about three hundred miles from the coast, but David could go no farther without a rest. The fever plagued him day after day until he was so weak he couldn't walk. The Makololo had to carry him on a litter made of branches.

A commander in the Portuguese army stationed in Tette

took David into his home. Here he rested, too weak to travel, until March 23.

When he was well enough, David went by canoe down the Zambezi to the east coast. He was going home. He had settled his Makololo friends on plantations in Tette where they could work and earn wages until his return.

From the port city of Quilimane he boarded a ship bound for England. He had not seen his country for sixteen years, or his own wife and children for five years.

He knew he would return. "Nothing but death will prevent my return," he had told the Makololo. But now he needed a rest. A long rest.

CHAPTER 8

The last five years had been hard for Mary Livingstone. Alone in England with her four children, sometimes not hearing news of her husband for long periods of time, she began to break down under the strain. But she also began to pray more and more. As she continued to pray, she began to feel peace, knowing that her Lord was able to take care of her husband, even if she could not. And then his letter came. David was coming home!

At the port of Southampton, David read the poem that Mary had written to him when she got his letter:

A hundred thousand welcomes, and it's time for you
  to come
From the far land of the foreigner, to your country
  and your home.
O long as we were parted, ever since you went away,
I never passed a dreamless night, or knew an easy day.
Do you think I would reproach you with the sorrows
  that I bore?
Since the sorrow is all over, now I have you here
  once more,
And there's nothing but the gladness and the love
  within my heart,

*And the hope so sweet and certain that again we'll
    never part.*
*A hundred thousand welcomes! How my heart is
    gushing o'er*
*With the love and joy and wonder thus to see your
    face once more.*
*How did I live without you these long, long years
    of woe?*
*It seems as if 'twould kill me to be parted from
    you now.*
*You'll never part me, Darling, there's a promise in
    your eye;*
*I may tend you while I'm living; you may watch me
    when I die;*
*And if death but kindly lead me to the blessed home
    on high,*
*What a hundred thousand welcomes will await you
    in the sky.*

David reached London on December 9, 1856. The Living-stones celebrated Christmas as a family for the first time in five years. David played with his children almost as if they had never been apart.

He had come home hoping for a time of quiet rest. But he didn't know that in the sixteen years he had been away all of England had made him a hero. Because of the journals he had sent home, and because of various accounts written about him by traveling friends and other journalists in Africa, his home country had never forgotten him. David had written several reports of the slave trade and had sent them to magazines and newspapers. These reports did more than anything else to stir up the anger of the nation, and of the whole world, against the evil of slavery. In America, where the great Civil War was only a few years away, the nation was growing sharply divided because of that very curse, slavery. In Africa, the war had already begun. British troops patroling the roads in the south had forced the slavers to move farther and farther north.

David had traveled over eleven thousand miles of African territory. In his travels, he had always made careful recordings of sites of hills, rivers, and lakes, many of them unknown to anyone before him. He had written hundreds of pages describing the country—the geography, climate, peoples, and the products that could be produced and traded to bring wealth to a poor nation. His work, in fact, led to the development of new maps of much of Africa!

The scientific world was fascinated by David's careful observations. The astronomer royal at Cape Town, Sir Thomas Maclear, said this of David's work:

"I never knew a man who, knowing scarcely anything of the method of making geographical observations, or laying down positions, became so soon an adept, that he could take the complete lunar observation, and altitudes for time, within fifteen minutes."

He went on to say that Livingstone's work in mapping the

course of the Zambezi River was "the finest specimen of sound geographical observation I ever met with. . . . I say, what that man has done is unprecedented. . . . You could go to any point across the entire continent, along Livingstone's track, and feel certain of your position."

David's life was now filled with speeches to universities, lectures to scientific groups, meetings with government officials, invitations to social gatherings, and even an invitation from the queen of England. He was made an honorary doctor of sciences by the University of Glasgow. And he had to write a book. A publisher named John Murray had convinced David that the world would want to read of his travels in Africa. He agreed, but only because he believed that the book could serve his Lord.

He hated to sit hour after hour writing. His heart yearned for the open plains, the dark forests, and sleeping under the bright African stars.

His public life held no enjoyment, either. He wished only to stay home with his family.

A close friend of the Livingstone family would later write the following:

Dr. Livingstone was very simple and unpretending, and used to be annoyed when he was made a lion of [fussed over]. Once a well-known gentleman, who was advertised to deliver a lecture the next day, called on him to pump him for material. The doctor sat rather quiet, and, without being rude, treated the gentleman to monosyllabic [one-syllable] answers. He could do that—could keep people at a distance when they wanted to make capital out of him. When the stranger had left, turning to my mother, [Livingstone] said, "I'll tell you anything you like to ask."

He never liked to walk in the streets for fear of being mobbed [because of his being so popular]. Once he was mobbed in Regent Street, and did not know how he was to escape, till he saw a cab, and took refuge in it. For the same reason it was painful for him to go to church. Once, being anxious to go with us, my father persuaded him that, as the seat at the top of our pew was under the galley, he would not be seen. As soon as he entered, he held down his head, and kept it covered with his hands all the time, but the preacher somehow caught sight of him, and rather unwisely, in his last prayer, adverted [referred] to him. This gave the people the knowledge that he was in the chapel, and after the service they came trooping toward him, even over pews, in their anxiety to see him and shake hands.

David's own letters to friends and family speak best for him:

Nowhere have I ever appeared as anything else but

a servant of God, who has simply followed the lead-
ings of His hand. My views of what is missionary
duty are not so contracted [limited] as those whose
ideal is a dumpy sort of man with a Bible under his
arm. I have labored in bricks and mortar, at the
forge and carpenter's bench, as well as in preaching
and medical practice. I feel that I am "not my own."
I am serving Christ when shooting a buffalo for my
men, or taking an astronomical observation, or
writing to one of His children. . . .

In December 1857, David was asked to speak at Oxford University. To the young men present he shared these thoughts:

"If you knew the satisfaction of performing such a
duty [as missionaries], as well as the gratitude to
God which the missionary must always feel, in being
chosen for so noble, so sacred a calling, you would
have no hesitation in embracing it. For my own part,
I have never ceased to rejoice that God has appoint-
ed me to such an office. People talk of the sacrifice I
have made in spending so much of my life in Africa.
Can that be called a sacrifice which is simply paid
back as a small part of a great debt owing to our
God, which we can never repay? . . . Say rather it is
a privilege.

"I beg to direct your attention to Africa: I know

that in a few years I shall be cut off in that country,
which is now open; do not let it be shut again! I go
back to Africa to try to make an open path for com-
merce and Christianity; do you carry out the work
which I have begun. I leave it with you!"

He had come home with only the clothes on his back. He would return to Africa as one of the most famous men in England, in all the world.

In February of 1858, he had been given a formal commission as Her Majesty's consul at Quilimane for the eastern coast and the independent districts in the interior, and commander of an expedition for exploring eastern and central Africa.

His mission was plain, he knew. He wanted to find some healthy place, high in altitude, in central Africa where missionaries could train natives to be teachers and preachers. He wanted to explore the jungles and rivers, to open up roads for trade—trade that would destroy slavery. Now he had the power of all of England at his command. David Livingstone's word would be law.

CHAPTER 9

Where was David Livingstone? All the world wanted to know. It was 1867, almost ten years since he had left England once again for Africa.

For several years, the reports were sent to England, telling of his progress through central Africa. But then one day all reports stopped. He seemed to have vanished. He had many enemies in Africa, to be sure. The Arab slave traders knew of David, and they had stayed clear of him as he traveled northward. The slave traders knew that England had declared war on the slave trade and that David carried the authority of the queen. But now what had happened to him? Was he captured or killed? Did he die in the bush from the African fever?

The world had learned of David's personal tragedy years earlier. His beloved Mary, who had traveled with him back to Africa, had become ill with the fever and had died.

Her death left David with a grief that he would carry for the rest of his life.

At Mary's death, David went north along the Rovuma River. He went almost aimlessly. He knew he must go on, to finish his work in this country. But now, though he still had his determination, his heart was gone. His heart, he felt, had been buried with Mary Livingstone in the town of Shupanca, where she had died.

Trudging along the trail by day, or sitting with his companions around a campfire by night, his thoughts had nowhere to go but onward. There would be no one waiting for him in Shupanca, in Kuruman, or in Mabotsa, the place of the marriage feast, where he and Mary had first lived. They would be reunited, he knew, but that reunion would not be for a long, long time. Mary was finally home, the home they never found together in this life, where they could rest from their wanderings and their work. When could he go home? He began to wonder now.

For now, there was only his work. On to the north. He wanted to reach Lake Nyassa. He believed that would be a good place to start an English colony. The land there was dry and healthy, he had heard, and the lake, which stretched north to south for over four hundred miles, offered fresh water.

For awhile, there was news of David's journey north. They went up the Shire River in a steamer. They passed pineapple, orange, and lemon trees. Antelopes and elephants came out of the forests to the river to drink. Monkeys swung and chattered in the trees.

They came to Murchison Falls and could go no farther by water. They landed and marched on, coming to Lake Shirwa, about fifty miles south of the huge Lake Nyassa. They stayed here for a few days and then began the climb into the Manganja hills. On September 16, 1859, David's party, forty-two in all, came to the waters of beautiful Lake Nyassa, stretching away to the north beyond sight. David Livingstone was the first white man ever to see this lake.

But though there was beauty here, there was evil, too. Arab sailing ships crossed Lake Nyassa, carrying newly captured slaves. Chained gangs of slaves were marched on paths along the shore.

David had an idea. A single British steamer carrying soldiers would stop the slave traffic on the lake. British and American settlements on the shores would put an end to the slave trade in this whole region. He wrote letters home to England. *Come and start a colony here,* he wrote. *Send missionaries, farmer, workers!*

He would have to wait a long time for answers to his letter, he knew. Meanwhile, he had a promise to fulfill. He sailed down the Shire to Tette, where he met his Makololo friends. It was a joyful reunion. "We knew you would return for us," they said. And they went back the way they had come, to Linyanti.

When David returned once again to Tette, England's answer to his letters was waiting for him—a light steamer called the *Pioneer.* On board was a band of missionaries sent by Oxford and Cambridge Universities, ready to go to work in the Shire valley. England had said yes to David's requests, and here was the first group of workers.

They steamed up the Shire to Murchison Falls, then walked the rest of the way to Lake Nyassa. On the way, they met a band of African slave drivers leading captive women and children. On seeing David, the slavers began shouting to one another and running off into the forest. Word was getting around: David Livingstone was out to stop the slave traffic.

The chained slaves cried and laughed and embraced their rescuers as David and his men sawed the forked sticks in two and unlocked the captives' bands. With the broken slave sticks, they made a fire and cooked breakfast for everyone. These freed slaves would become the first members of Lake Nyassa's mission church.

Livingstone then left these missionaries and traveled north to the city of Zanzibar on the east coast. Here were the worst horrors of all. Slaves were sold in the marketplaces, like cattle, the buyers prodding their ribs and pulling open their mouths to look at their teeth. The day David arrived, an Arab ship landed with three hundred more slaves.

David was sick of the sounds and sights of Zanzibar. He rented a light ship and sailed south again. On foot and along narrow paths through grass taller than their heads David and his men traveled, but all the villages they came to were empty. The huts were burned, the gardens uprooted, the people all gone—to the slavers.

They went on, to the north again. Their food ran low. After several weeks, all they had to eat was cornmeal soaked in goats' milk. Then one night the goats were stolen. On another night David's medicine chest was stolen.

Without his medicine, he was constantly suffering from fever. Because the slavers had destroyed all the crops behind them as they went on, there was no food for the Livingstone party. With only the dry corn to eat, David lost his teeth, one by one.

They had to go on. There were no civilized settlements in this area. David needed to reach Ujiji, an Arab settlement on the east shore of Lake Tanganyika, about three hundred miles west of Lake Nyassa. From there, he hoped to receive news from his country and his children. And to rest.

But there was a long way to go. David became so sick that finally he had to be carried, once again, in a litter. Only five men were with him now; the rest had run off. Along the trail, the dangers were increasing day by day. The natives who had not been captured were out seeking revenge. Any foreigner was their enemy, they believed. Although until now they were afraid to come near him, the Arab slave traders wanted David —dead.

Suddenly all were his enemies. None was his friend.

In England the reports came in: David Livingstone was lost. . .or dead. The news reached America. Was it true? One man decided to find out.

CHAPTER 10

He was an American; that was clear. The American flag rode at the head of the procession. He wore light-colored clothes, a bush hat, and knee-high boots. Behind him came about two hundred native porters, wearing packs. Oxen pulled wagons loaded with canvas bundles.

They came up the street of Ujiji. The American looked slowly from right to left, scanning faces of blacks and Arabs. A white man now came out of a little house just up the street. He was skinny and bearded. His face and hands were almost as brown as those of the native men with him, who were dressed in English clothes. The white man's clothes hung loosely on his frame and were patched here and there but clean.

They met in the street. The American took off his hat and bowed slightly to the bearded man. Then he said, "Dr. Livingstone, I presume?"

When David had not been heard from for a long time, one man wanted to find out why. Gordon Bennett, publisher of the *New York Herald,* decided to find David. He would spend any amount necessary and would find him dead or alive. If alive, the *Herald* would be the first to report the news to the world. If dead, he would bring his bones home for burial and report that to the world.

Bennett sent a telegram on October 16, 1869, to Madrid, Spain, to one of his paper's traveling correspondents, Henry Morton Stanley. *Find Livingstone,* Bennett said, *dead or alive. Take whatever you need; spend as much as you need; take as long as you need. Just find him.*

For some reason, Bennett sent Stanley on a roundabout journey: first to Constantinople (today Istanbul, Turkey), Palestine (Israel and the West Bank), and Egypt, then to India, before landing in Zanzibar in January, 1871.

Stanley's expedition inland was massive. Almost two hundred men in five caravans set out for Ujiji on Lake Tanganyika. From what he had learned, Stanley guessed that Ujiji was the last place David had been seen.

Stanley's party went slowly. Because of trouble on the roads—Arabs and native tribes were at war—Stanley had to turn far out of the way and travel south. The journey took from March to November.

Finally they reached Ujiji. Stanley later wrote of his meeting with David Livingstone:

As I advanced slowly toward him, I noticed he was pale, looking wearied, had a gray beard, wore a bluish cap with a faded gold band around it, had on a red-sleeved waistcoat and a pair of gray tweed trousers. I would have run to him, only I was a coward in the presence of such a mob—would have embraced him, only he, being an Englishman, I did not know how he would receive me; so I did what cowardice and false pride suggested was the best thing—walked deliberately to him, took off my hat, and said, "Dr. Livingstone, I presume?" "Yes," said he, with a kind smile, lifting his cap slightly. I replaced my hat on my head, and he puts on his cap, and we both grasp hands, and then I say aloud—"I thank God, Doctor, I have been permitted to see you." He answered, "I feel thankful that I am here to welcome you."

David was indeed thankful. Stanley brought stores of food, clothes, sheets of copper, a tent, a boat, a bathtub, cooking pots, medicine, tools, books, paper, guns, and—most precious to David—letters. Stanley had brought a whole mailbag full. David ransacked the bag, digging through letters from friends and government officials, until he found what he was looking for. With tears in his eyes, he read the two letters from his children. (Somehow, Livingstone's mail had not gone in and out of Ujiji. He later learned that Arab slavers had held his mail so that he would die alone here, abandoned by the world.)

Stanley would stay here for over four months. The two would become close friends. They would sit and talk for hours each day. Of most value to David was news of the world. Stanley, too, was fascinated by all that David told him of his travels in Africa. He gave Stanley his journal, with all his personal and scientific notes, written from his arrival at Zanzibar on January 28, 1866, to February 20, 1872. He asked Stanley to take this back with him.

With good food and new medicine, David's health returned quickly. He had just got back from a long journey, he said, and had come into Ujiji almost dead. "You have brought me new life," he told Stanley, over and over.

Stanley came to love and respect David Livingstone. He would later write:

You may take any point in Dr. Livingstone's character, and analyze it carefully, and I would challenge any man to find a fault in it. . . . His gentleness never forsakes him: His hopefulness never deserts him: No harassing anxieties, distraction of mind; long separation from home and kindred, can make him complain. . . .

There is a good-natured abandon about Livingstone which was not lost on me. Whenever he began to laugh, there was a contagion about it that compelled me to imitate him. It was a laugh. . .of the whole man from head to heel. . . .

Another thing that especially attracted my attention was his wonderful retentive memory. If we remember the many years he has spent in Africa, deprived of books, we may well think it an uncommon memory that can recite whole poems from Byron, Burns, Tennyson, Longfellow, Whittier, and Lowell. . . .

*His religion is not of the theoretical kind, but it is
a constant, earnest, sincere practice. It is neither
demonstrative nor loud, but manifests itself in a
quiet, practical way, and is always at work. . . .*

*From being thwarted and hated in every possible
way upon his first arrival at Ujiji, he has, through
his uniform kindness and mild, pleasant temper, won
all hearts. I observed that mutual respect was paid
to him. Even the Mohammedans never passed his
house without calling to pay their compliments, and
to say, "The blessing of God rest on you." Each
Sunday morning he gathers his little flock around
him and reads prayers and a chapter from the Bible,
in a natural, unaffected, and sincere tone and afterward delivers a short address in the Kisqwahilil language, about the subject read to them, which is listened to with evident interest and attention.*

The day finally came for Henry Stanley to leave.

*March 14th—We had a sad breakfast together. I
could not eat, my heart was too full; neither did my
companion seem to have an appetite. We found
something to do which kept us together longer. At
eight o'clock I was not gone, and I had thought to
have been off at five A.M. . . . We walked side by
side; the men lifted their voices in a song. I took*

long looks at Livingstone to impress his features
thoroughly on my memory. . . . "Now, my dear doc-
tor, the best friends must part. You have come far
enough; let me beg of you to turn back." "Well,"
Livingstone replied, "I will say this to you: You have
done what few men could do—far better than some
great travelers I know. And I am grateful to you for
what you have done for me. God guide you and
bless you, my friend."—"And may God bring you
safe back to us all, my dear friend. Farewell!"—
"Farewell!"

"Susi, bring my watch," came the faint voice from inside the hut. Susi, David's trusted native friend for many years, went in and gently laid the watch in his palm.

They had just come to this village called Ilala. They had been traveling for weeks. David had wanted to make one more journey, this one to find the great river called Luapula that he had heard many rumors about. This river, it was said, was the source of the Nile River. No one had ever found the source of the Nile.

But here they had to stop. David was so weak with a new attack of fever that he could not go on. He lay now in the cool darkness of the hut, too weak even to lift his arm. Susi sat by his friend. Night came. Just after eleven o'clock, Livingstone spoke again.

"Is this the Luapula?"

"No," Susi said softly. "We are in Chitambo's village near the Molilamo."

"How many days is it to the Luapula?"

"I think it is three days, Master."

David was silent now. Susi waited until his master was asleep, then went to his own hut.

Just before dawn, Susi was awakened. "Come to Bwana [master]," said the boy. "I am afraid."

Susi and three others went quickly to David's hut. His candle had burned low. In its dim, flickering light, the four men saw the still form of their master and friend kneeling by his bed, his head buried in his hands on his pillow.

The men waited, silent, in the doorway. They never disturbed their master while he was praying. But how did he find the strength to get out of bed and kneel? Hours earlier, he could barely talk.

They waited and waited. David's candle went out. Susi lit another and went softly to David and touched his cheek. Then the tears that he had been holding back 'til now streamed down his face. His master's cheek was cold.

David Livingstone was home.

In Westminster Abbey in London where David Livingstone is buried, you can find a headstone with the following words:

Brought by faithful hands over land and over sea,
Here Rests DAVID LIVINGSTONE, Missionary Traveler,

Philanthropist. Born March 19, 1813, at Blantyre, Lanarkshire. Died May 4th, 1873, at Chitambo's Village, Ilala. For thirty years his life was spent in an unwearied effort to evangelize the native races, to explore the undiscovered secrets, And abolish the desolating slave trade of central Africa, where, with his last words, he wrote: "All I can say in my solitude is, May Heaven's rich blessing come down on every-one—American, English, Turk—who will help to heal the open sore of the world."

GLADYS AYLWARD

COURAGEOUS MISSIONARY TO CHINA

by Sam Wellman

CHAPTER 1

On February 24, 1929, Gladys Aylward turned twenty-seven years old. For years, she had worked as a parlor maid in wealthy homes in London. She actually lived in the mansions of her employers. She had never married, but that was not the reason she was unhappy. She was unhappy because more than anything else in life she wanted to go to China as a missionary. She had even managed once to enroll as a student in the China Inland Mission, a famous missionary society in London that sent missionaries to China. But they had given up on Gladys. They had told her she was too old to learn the Chinese language. She had never felt such a sense of failure. She felt she was just a mousey little parlormaid.

In her tiny bedroom she would cry, "Use me, God! Oh, please use me. . . ."

How she wanted to go to China. She even managed to get a job as a parlor maid in the house of Sir Francis Younghusband. Sir Francis was an explorer famous for traveling all the way across China to the country of Tibet, where he was the first westerner to enter the "Forbidden City" of the Dalai Lama! Now Sir Francis lived in London and wrote books about his great adventures. Gladys felt honored to just work in the great explorer's house. But it didn't satisfy her urge to go to China. It made her want to go to China even more.

One day she was talking to a friend in her church group. The friend mentioned an elderly missionary in China named Jeannie Lawson. For some reason Jeannie was unable to get help in her mission work. She was virtually alone in her work and afraid her work would end. So Jeannie Lawson had written friends in London pleading for someone to come to China and help her.

"That's me!" yelped Gladys.

Gladys was so excited that her heart was pounding like a hammer. She immediately wrote Jeannie Lawson and volunteered. Meanwhile she had to figure out how she would get to China. Travel to China by plane in those days was not possible. When she inquired at a travel agency about a ticket on a ship to China, she was flabbergasted. It cost far more money than she had saved. But she was astonished to learn that if she crossed the North Sea in a small ship to Holland she could catch a train that would take her all the way across Europe, then across the vast country of Russia and eventually to China! The cost of such a ticket was only half what the ticket on a ship cost.

Still, the agent discouraged her. The agent explained that local leaders called warlords controlled much of China. "The warlords in China are often fighting the Russians along the border of China and Russia. The far end of the railroad could be very dangerous."

Nevertheless Gladys persisted. "Here's a down payment." The agent relented and took her tiny amount of money, probably thinking she would never be able to save enough to pay the rest, anyway. But Gladys began to save every penny. She took extra jobs on her days off to make more money. She began selling her possessions. She even sold everything in her "hope chest," those valuable items that young women in those days kept for their future marriage. If Jeannie Lawson wrote that Gladys could come, Gladys had to have the money for a train ticket. One day Gladys received a letter covered with bright, colorful stamps. She couldn't read one symbol on the stamps, but Gladys knew who had sent the letter. Her stomach felt like it was full of fluttering butterflies as she tore open the envelope.

"Yes!" she gasped. "I must only reach a town called Tientsin on the coast of China and then write Jeannie Lawson that I have arrived!"

God was going to use her! Her dream had come true.

In a daze, she quit her job and traveled to Edmonton in the north of London. Her parents lived in a small red-brick house at 67 Cheddington Road. Rosalind, her "Mum," still bustled about the kitchen when she wasn't at the missions preaching against the evil of alcohol. Thomas, her dad, still clomped in at nightfall in his heavy boots and his mailman's uniform. When Gladys had been a child, she had seen open fields out their lace-curtained windows. Beyond their flowery hedge, horses had clopped along the cobblestone street, pulling carts. Their drivers had loudly hawked milk, vegetables, bread, and a dozen other things. But it wasn't that way in late 1929. London

—one of the most heavily populated cities in the world—crowded in all around Cheddington Road and brought smoke-spewing automobiles and trucks.

"Seems odd to me that you can take a train to China," mumbled Dad, who looked sick with worry.

"Three weeks and I'll be there, Dad!" gushed Gladys.

"Won't it be winter in Russia?" he fretted.

"I'll be on the train, Dad!"

So her parents helped her get ready for the trip. She packed two huge suitcases. One was crammed full with her clothing, a passport, and her Bible. In every nook and cranny she added hard-boiled eggs and packets of cookies and crackers. The other suitcase was stuffed only with food—cans of sardines, corned beef, and beans, as well as jars of bouillon cubes and powdered coffee. She also packed a tiny alcohol stove, for Gladys planned on eating that food during her very long train trip. Her mother wisely talked her into also carrying a heavy coat and an old fur muffler to put around her neck.

After Gladys left London behind, she buried her face in the fur muffler and let the tears flow. Would she ever see her Mum and Dad again? Sister Violet? Brother Lawrence? England? When she finally left the small ship that crossed the North Sea, she boarded the train in Holland. The train people told her she would not change trains again until she reached Russia. She was in a compartment that she shared with just a few others. She worried a little as she crossed Germany. In 1929 Germany was being taken over by the Nazis. Their leader,

Adolf Hitler, was on the radio all the time screaming terrible things. He seemed to hate everything not German. The British people could not figure out if he was just a stupid politician or someone really dangerous.

At the Russian border, Gladys had to transfer to a different train because the Russian trains moved on rails that were closer together. But she still had a compartment that she shared with a few others. Few Russians seemed able to speak English. Gladys was also struck by the poverty of the Russians. Russia was controlled by Communists. Many in Britain thought the Communists were improving the lives of the Russians, but Gladys saw they were not. Never had she seen people who looked so downcast. The Russian people were very fearful, too. And Gladys began to worry. Perhaps her long journey through Russia would not be so pleasant. . . .

After several days in Russia, Gladys could see few people in the countryside. The train rolled across the snowy vastness of that part of Russia called Siberia. One day a man in a business suit entered her compartment. He bowed slightly. "Madam, the conductor asked me to speak to you. Your ticket is to China. The train no longer goes on to China."

"Yes, Sir. Thank you so much for informing me." Gladys nodded politely, but her heart jumped.

Was she really going to be stopped? Were the Russians fighting the Chinese warlords? Well, in any event, she would just stay on the train, no matter what. This wasn't her war. One by one, as the train continued on its journey, the other passengers got off at their stops, each stop more mountainous than the one before. Only soldiers got on the train now. Soon Gladys seemed not just the only woman aboard but the only person who was not a soldier or a train crewman. The noisy soldiers watched her as she periodically opened her suitcase to retrieve a cracker or a cookie. She didn't offer them any food. They had their own food rations, and she didn't dare run out of food before she reached China. The cold, forbidding mountains they were passing through now frightened her.

At the railway station called Chita, a crewman on the train came into her compartment. "Must leave now. . . ," he labored in rough English.

"Certainly not!" she snapped.

He shrugged and left. The train continued on. Finally in the night it stopped. Voices erupted. Soldiers tramped up and down the corridor. Doors slammed. The soldiers in her compartment left abruptly. Then the train was silent. It was scary. All that silence in the train, after days of constant clamor. Gladys tiptoed into the corridor. In every direction the train was dark. She had the unmistakable feeling she was now really alone. She went back into her compartment and opened the outside door. *Pop, pop, pop* went the night air.

"Firecrackers?" she mulled as she listened. Chinese were famous for firecrackers. Then reality hit her. What a fool she was. "Those sharp pops are gunfire!"

She left the train and lugged her belongings down the platform toward a distant fire. By the fire she found the train's crewmen, including the one who had asked her in Chita to leave the train.

He shook his head. "See. Train stop here. Go back Chita."

After much waving of his hands, the man convinced Gladys the train would stay there until it was needed to take wounded Russian soldiers back to Chita and beyond. The wait could be days or even weeks! Gladys could scarcely believe the turn of events. But she believed the man. Soon—in the dead of the Russian winter and in mountain country—she was actually trudging back to Chita. She followed the train track, wading through the shallow snow between the rails. She stumbled over the gapped wooden ties that the rails were spiked into. But she couldn't walk in the deep snow outside the rails. After awhile the fire back on the platform was no longer visible. The night was black. Once she was startled to realize she was walking through a tunnel. She fought the silly fear that a train might be coming.

"Oh, God Almighty, give me courage," she prayed.

Courage did come to drive away her increasing dread. Finally, in one small tunnel, she stopped. The tunnel was the closest thing to shelter she would find. She used her alcohol stove to fix a cup of coffee. She slowly munched two crackers. That would have to do. Fatigue overwhelmed her. Wrapped in her coat, she huddled under her luggage tented into a crude hut. She was too tired to realize what distant barking might mean in the Siberian wilderness. Dogs? Out here? But when she awoke in the clean, dawn light, she realized the terror that lurked behind that barking.

"Wolves!"

All day long she trudged along the mountainous, winding track. Snow and great pine trees stretched to the horizons. Her strength began to fail. She must reach Chita before nightfall. She couldn't take another Siberian night with its icy cold and slavering wolves. Finally, in early evening, she saw distant dots of light shining like gold. By nightfall she reached the train platform in Chita. Once again she confounded the railway officials.

Nyet! Nyet! Nyet! boomed their Russian voices.

Except for *nyet,* which meant "no," Gladys understood nothing else they said. Soon soldiers came to escort her inside the station. After one day inside the station, a government official came who spoke some English. He arranged for her passage on a railway line that went around the fighting. After several days on that train, Gladys heard a stop announced that she recognized.

"Vladivostok!" yelled the train official.

"Oh, praise God," murmured Gladys.

Vladivostok was a port on the Sea of Japan. But how was Gladys supposed to get to China? Gladys was escorted to a hotel by an official in suit and tie. His face was sour and his questions in English were bold.

"Why don't you wish to stay here and work for our great Communist society?" asked the man. "Why go waste your life on that bunch of yellow barbarians to the south? You are white, like me. You are civilized, like me. Our great Communist society can use bright people like you."

Gladys was so disgusted with his racial slurs she broke off the conversation. She had to find a way to China. A woman timidly approached her in the lobby of the hotel and warned her in English she had just been talking to a man in the Russian secret police. The secret police were very dangerous. She told Gladys what to do. Soon Gladys was able to slip away from the hotel and buy passage on a cargo ship to Japan. It was her only way out. That was the first time she noticed the Communists had altered her passport. They had changed her occupation from "missionary" to "machinist"! So Gladys suspected they were going to send her to some work camp as a machinist and lie that she had volunteered to anyone who ever asked what became of her.

The woman who helped her appeared again.

"Why are you taking such a risk for me?" asked Gladys.

"Not all Russians are bad," the woman whispered tearfully. "Hurry. Leave." Abruptly she was gone.

Gladys had almost no money left. The Japanese captain of the ship seemed to take her on just so he could say he had helped a British citizen in great trouble. Maybe the British someday would be able to return the favor.

"Praise God for your kindness," she said.

"Praise Japan," he snapped.

Three days later, the cargo ship docked at a small port named Tsuruga in Japan. Within hours Gladys was onshore, sitting in a restaurant with a very young man from the British consulate. He was bewildered. Whatever was he going to do with Gladys? British citizens just simply did not get themselves marooned in this small port on the west coast of Japan.

"The captain of the cargo ship told me to go to Kobe," she said forcefully. "There I can get a ship to China."

"Kobe?" His face lit up. "We must get you a train ticket right away!"

He was so eager to remove this possible stain on his promising career that he bought the ticket himself. Gladys soon found herself on a train again, gazing out the window at the Japanese countryside. Other than their hostility toward China, Gladys knew very little about the Japanese. The Japanese themselves seemed very polite. In Kobe, English missionaries helped Gladys arrange her ticket on a steamer to China. Soon Gladys boarded a steamer that sailed out into the Pacific Ocean. Gladys became more excited with each passing day. She spent more time on deck squinting at the distant horizon. One day a dark blue fringe materialized on the western horizon. The fringe grew and greened.

"China, at long last!" she gasped.

CHAPTER 3

Tientsin made the ports of Vladivostok and Tsuruga, even Kobe, look like country villages. Streets teemed with Chinese. While riding in a rickshaw to the headquarters of a missionary society, Gladys was startled to remember how disappointed she had been as a teenage girl with her own tiny stature and black hair. But now here she was among short, black-haired people. She felt not disappointment but utter joy.

"Jeannie Lawson said I was to wait here until she sent a guide for me," she told a woman who greeted her at the missionary society.

"Jeannie Lawson?" gasped the woman. "Oh, gracious me, that could take a very long time. You see, we would have to get in touch with her. Then she would have to get in touch with us. . . ."

"But. . ."

"You must just go on ahead and find her."

"Find her?"

"Yes, she is a bit of a rebel, you see."

"An elderly missionary woman?"

The woman smiled indulgently. "Jeannie Lawson travels around in the far province of Shansi pretty much as she pleases."

The missionary society took Gladys in while they searched

for someone dependable to take her to Shansi. In the meantime she explored. Villages and towns were walled. The smaller villages consisted of one main street lined on both sides by walled buildings. So each building was a small fortress in itself. A visitor went in one gate of the village and went out the other. At night the gates were locked. The poorest of the poor lived outside the walls. The missionaries told her villages all over China were built on that plan, a plan that must have gone back thousands of years of mistrust. Walls were everywhere.

"Walls, walls, walls," said one missionary pointedly.

Gladys also began to learn about the Chinese language. She prayed that God would allow her, at nearly thirty years of age, to learn Chinese. It was certainly a peculiar language to any person who spoke English. Words were generally one syllable. The written language was understood all over China by those who could read. But different areas pronounced the words differently. So China had seven spoken dialects! A person who could not read could not understand a person from another area.

"Don't look so worried, Gladys," said one missionary. "Here and in Shansi the Chinese speak the dialect of Mandarin. In fact, three hundred million Chinese speak Mandarin!"

Gladys listened willingly to this information about language, but her head was spinning. She was pleased, though, when the missionary society finally arranged for her to travel to Shansi with a Chinese Christian. Mr. Lu, a businessman, wore a dark blue robe and a fedora hat. The two rode a train that chugged across a plain of gold-stubbled rice paddies. The rice had already been harvested. Mr. Lu explained that the locals also farmed peanuts, beans, and corn. On deeply rutted roads two-wheel carts rattled along, pulled by shaggy ponies.

"Blue seems to be everyone's favorite color in China," commented Gladys about the clothing she saw.

"Blue is the cheapest dye for clothes," offered Mr. Lu. "The blue dye is made from a root found all over China."

Just before one nightfall she saw the great towers and walls of Beijing rise ahead. Within the city were the great palaces of the old emperors. Gladys got little more than a glimpse. Outside Beijing she saw the Great Wall of China itself. It looked just like Sir Francis Younghusband had described it in one his books. He wrote, "As far as the eyes could see, ran this wonderful wall, going down the side of one hill, up the next, over its summit and down the other side again. . .thirty or forty feet high, of solid stone, and fifteen feet or so thick. . .with towers every few hundred feet. . ."

"The Great Wall is over two thousand years old and runs for fifteen hundred miles east to west," informed Mr. Lu. "Its original purpose was to keep out invaders from the north."

Three days later the railway track ran out. Now they rode on busses. They spent the nights at inns. The inns were always walled, and their entrance gates to the main street closed at night. In the open-aired central yard of the inn were busses and carts. Along one wall were stalls for horses and mules. On the other side, the guests were housed. In one large room, they ate bowls of steaming rice and vegetables. Onions, bamboo sprouts, water chestnuts, yams, cabbage, and carrots were flavored with garlic, anise, and ginger. Gladys had heard of delicacies like sugared lotus seeds, bird's nest soup, and limed eggs, but nothing like that was served at any inn she could afford. No form of meat made the menu where she stayed, either. Nor were bread products known in these rice-eating areas, she learned from Mr. Lu. Occasionally before the gate was locked, villagers would flock into the inn to look at Gladys.

"What are they saying?" Gladys would ask. But Mr. Lu seemed too embarrassed to translate.

But one greeting—*Chi-la fan ma?*—she heard over and over again. He explained it literally meant, "Have you eaten?" but it was intended to be a polite greeting. Gladys guessed the expression stemmed from the Chinese obsession with food, because they rarely had enough to eat. She never saw overweight Chinese. The proper response to the polite greeting was "Yes, I have eaten"—in Chinese, *Chi-la.*

The guests slept on a *kang.* This was a raised mud or brick platform under which hot air was billowed from a stove maintained in the kitchen. The *kang* was warm but very hard, in spite of a mat that covered it.

Mr. Lu told Gladys, "Everyone in colder regions of China sleeps on *kangs.*"

Some of the travelers used bricks for pillows, if one could call such a hard thing a pillow! Often the inn had only one enormous room for guests. There was no privacy. Everyone slept on a communal *kang* under blankets. Except for removing shoes, no one undressed. Gladys was quick to notice that in the morning everyone turned their shoes over and shook them before putting them on again. So Gladys shook her shoes, too. One morning something dropped out of a man's shoe. The man swatted it with his shoe.

"Scorpion," gulped Gladys.

About the only change in the long trip that Gladys noticed was the disappearance of bowls of rice at the inns and the appearance of bowls of thick, doughy noodles. They had passed into wheat country. One month after leaving Tientsin, their route veered up into the foothills of mountains. Gladys had arrived in Tsechow, an important trading center. Here Gladys felt she was in ancient China. Trucks were there, but great ambling, loose-lipped camels were there, too. These ancient beasts brought tobacco, silks, and other fabrics across the lowlands, then headed back that same direction with coal, ironware, and cotton. Mr. Lu left Gladys at the missionary house of the China Inland Mission. An elderly Mrs. Smith peppered her with questions about England. But where was Jeannie Lawson?

"Oh, Jeannie," said Mrs. Smith, smiling. "She's off in the mountains. Yangcheng, we heard."

"Will I travel there by bus?"

"Dear me, no. You'll be finding no busses in the mountains. All transport is by mule on trails as old as civilization. Yangcheng is on an age-old mule trail that runs all through the high country of Shansi. And the province of Shansi is as large as the entire country of England!"

"China certainly changes one's perspective," gasped Gladys. "How long have you lived here?"

"Oh, for almost fifty years. . ."

"Fifty years! You must have been among the very first missionaries."

"Yes, my husband was one of the group of missionaries some people call the 'Cambridge Seven.' "

"The Cambridge Seven! Then you must be Mrs. Stanley Smith!"

"Oh, Dear, you mustn't carry on so."

Gladys went to bed numb. She had been talking to a woman almost legendary in missionary circles. It wasn't as if Gladys hadn't seen celebrated people before. After all, she had worked in the wealthiest parts of London. But now she was among God's servants. And Mrs. Smith treated her, Gladys the parlor maid, as an equal!

"Surely this is a great gift to me from God," reflected Gladys. "Hallelujah!"

The next morning Mrs. Smith sent for a mule *shanza*. She also advised Gladys that her Western clothes were no longer appropriate. It was never advisable in the mountains to advertise one was a foreigner. Soon Gladys was attired in standard

Chinese wear: high-collared blue jacket and blue trousers. She also learned they simply added layer after layer of the same style of clothing as the weather demanded. Naturally each additional layer had to be a larger size.

"Up in Yangcheng you will know a 'four-layer' day soon enough," advised Mrs. Smith. "And the clothing will be quilted and padded with cotton besides."

That's only an inkling of unknowns yet to come, reflected Gladys. And when the muleteer and his assistant arrived outside the missionary house with the mule *shanza,* it certainly was nothing like she had imagined. . . .

CHAPTER 4

Lying on the ground were two poles eight feet long and separated by two three-foot crossbars. The two long poles and the crossbars supported a network of interlaced rope. On this network was a mattress. Soon Gladys was sitting on the mattress. The muleteer arched matting over Gladys to form a canopy. Her two bags he placed ahead of her. The muleteer's assistant led a saddled mule to the front end of the two poles.

Gladys tried to peer out at Mrs. Smith. "But shouldn't the *shanza*. . ."

Suddenly the front end of the poles shot up in the air so violently that Gladys thought she was going to be launched into space. The muleteer and his assistant dropped the front ends of the poles into grooves on the saddle. Barely hanging on, Gladys thought she heard another mule being brought up behind her. Suddenly the rear end of the poles rose in space and then plopped down. Gladys didn't have to look to know the poles had settled into grooves on the second mule's saddle.

"Muleteers can be a bit rough at times," commented Mrs. Smith. Suddenly the whole contraption lurched forward. Mrs. Smith shouted, "Bye, Gladys."

The rumbly ride smoothed out as the strides of the two mules fell into unison. Gladys relaxed. When her feet began to elevate, she realized the mules were clopping up a rocky trail. After awhile she managed to peer out from under the canopy. There seemed not enough room to leave the *shanza* without stepping into space and falling hundreds of feet down a vertical cliff.

"God, protect me," she prayed.

The mountains seemed bare rock and wisps of grass. At nightfall they stopped at an inn, then continued the next morning. Her muscles ached from the rolling and pitching of the mule *shanza,* but she was elated. Her long journey was almost over, and the sight that greeted her after one bend in the trail was more wonderful than anything she had ever imagined. The mountain beyond was not bare but terraced with crops of corn and millet and wheat. Dark clumps of green signaled groves of trees. Yangcheng seemed an ancient fairy tale told to her for the first time. It clung to the south side of a mountain, to bathe itself in the sun. Soft tan walls grew out of the mountainside like an eagle's nest. Tiled roofs rose tantalizingly above the walls. The stacked roofs with their curled-up eaves seemed magical.

"At long last I am here. . . ."

But Gladys never entered the walls of Yangcheng. Near the East Gate the muleteer led the *shanza* off to a cluster of dwellings—the abodes of the poor—hugging the mountainside below the walls of the village. Suddenly they stopped. Gladys peered from under her canopy. They were in front of a large walled building with a front door hanging askew on one hinge.

Gladys murmured, "Could this possibly be. . . ?"

Whomp!

The muleteer and his assistant had loosed the rear ends of the poles, and the *shanza* had dropped like a rock to the ground. Gladys realized the front ends would soon be falling, too, so she scrambled out of the *shanza*. A woman as tiny as Gladys, dressed in a blue robe and pants, faced her with her hands on her hips. The woman had snow-white hair. Small, round "granny" spectacles did not soften her fierce, sky blue eyes.

Chi-la fan ma? asked the white-haired woman.

Chi-la, blurted Gladys. "Thank you very much for asking, but no, I haven't really eaten. I'm starved. Well, what I mean to say is. . ."

"You are British?" interrupted the woman in barely recognizable English. "Who would you be then?"

"Why, I'm Gladys Aylward. Are you Jeannie Lawson?"

"You'll be coming in then," said the white-haired woman brusquely and scurried inside the building.

Gladys passed through the doorway and entered the courtyard. The building was two-storied, spacious, and sturdy but very littered. Jeannie Lawson pointed at this pile of rubbish and at that broken door, chattering all the while as if Gladys had known her for a lifetime. Her accent was very thick, shaped by fifty years in China. Sometimes Gladys strained almost in agony to understand what Jeannie Lawson said, only to realize she was speaking Chinese.

"So this is your missionary house," mused Gladys during

one of Jeannie Lawson's few pauses.

"Maybe and maybe not," replied Jeannie Lawson stubbornly. "I've just rented it. I could only afford it because the locals think it's haunted. I know you're burning up with curiosity to know what the rent is. . ."

"Why, no. . . ," Gladys weighed her words.

But then Gladys was distracted by a commotion outside. She wandered over to the only door that opened to the street. She stepped outside. A ball of mud struck her shoulder and she heard children scream, *Lao-yang-kwei! Lao-yang-kwei!* and scuffle off. She turned to Jeannie Lawson.

Lao-yang-kwei. They called you a 'foreign devil,' " sighed Jeannie Lawson as if it happened a hundred times a day. *Mu yu fadze,* she continued, then translated, "It can't be helped." She sighed again. "They are even more frightened of me because of my white hair. Very few Chinese have white hair. Be thankful those urchins couldn't find any stones."

"Are they all like that?" asked Gladys uneasily.

"Not all." Jeannie clapped her hands and screamed, "Yang!" An elderly Chinese man appeared out of a room Gladys had not examined yet. "This is Yang, our cook," explained Jeannie. "Yang is a Christian. He is not afraid of foreign devils." She fired some Chinese at Yang. Yang laughed.

Jeannie showed Gladys into the only room besides their kitchen that she had managed to clean. In the room were a table and two chairs. On the wall that the room shared with the kitchen was a *kang* with its bedding. Boxes were stacked near the opposite wall. Awhile later Yang returned with a bowl of steamed vegetables and doughy noodles. The food was for Gladys. She felt much better after that.

"Thank You, Lord," she prayed that night. "I can't wait to get started."

There was one thing Gladys was truly an expert at. Cleaning. Even Jeannie, who seemed impressed by almost nothing, paused once in awhile with her hands on her hips to marvel. Gladys transformed the building. The inn had several smaller rooms, but most importantly it had three very large rooms with *kangs* that would make excellent dormitories. Yang was able to help Gladys repair the doors. Gladys never doubted for a moment the building would make a most excellent missionary house. Of course, getting the Chinese to enter the building was another problem. Her few excursions outside were met by angry villagers. The only thing that kept them from attacking, according to Jeannie, was their fear of the local Mandarin—or ruler—who had decreed that there was to be no violence done on foreigners.

Soon Gladys had the building ready for many occupants. "When are we going to open our missionary house?" she asked.

"I'm still thinking on it."

Jeannie was cantankerous. Sometimes she seemed to be teetering on the edge of sanity. But how could Gladys know what memories might torment the old missionary? So Gladys waited. One day, she was watching one mule train after another mule train plod into the East Gate of Yangcheng. Mule train after mule train plodded out of the gate going the other direction. A mule was as large and powerful as a horse but as gentle as a donkey. In the trains, the mules were loaded down with coal and cotton and metal goods. Because mules would taint grain with their smell, the train also consisted of men walking on foot, laden with sacks of wheat, millet, and corn. A train could consist of six to ten mules and twice that many men. Jeannie said these men were like sailors. A complete circuit of the trade route took about three months. It struck Gladys that the muleteers and their many helpers were just about the only ones who tied the entire province together.

"You know," Gladys said to Jeannie, "if you could convert a muleteer he could carry the gospel all over Shansi."

"How did you figure that out!" Jeannie looked as if Gladys had slapped her. "Oh, why didn't I tell you sooner? Now you'll think it was your idea."

Now Gladys was sure Jeannie suffered from some mental disease. She had worked among too many people too long not to recognize it. The disease (which would someday be called Alzheimer's disease) affected rich and poor alike. Some of the afflicted could be unpredictably belligerent. A few afflicted victims raged. Yes, Gladys had seen it before. It never got better. This suspected illness became a great worry to her. What if something happened to Jeannie? The old missionary was seventy-five years old, anyway. How would Gladys ever manage alone in Yangcheng? People ran from her, spat at her, threw mud at her. Gladys was a foreign devil. . . .

"The name for our inn," said Jeannie abruptly, "is the Inn of Eight Happinesses. You see, I thought of it first."

Gladys later learned the eight Chinese happinesses were devotion, virtue, gentleness, tolerance, loyalty, truth, beauty, and love. So their inn was ready to open. The rooms were clean. They had hay for the mules. Yang was ready to cook. Only one thing was lacking: customers. Yang had spread the word among the villagers, but no one came. Jeannie and Gladys took turns standing at their door and screaming in Chinese at the passing muleteers.

"We have no bedbugs," they shouted. "We have no fleas! Good, good, good. Come! Come! Come!" But nothing seemed to draw the mules or muleteers into the inn.

One morning Jeannie announced, "These trains will have to be led in by force."

Gladys couldn't believe Jeannie's bizarre plan. And Gladys was the one who had to carry it out. Nevertheless, she watched for the first muleteer that day who appeared to be gawking about for an inn. Then she dashed out to lunge at the lead mule and grab one of the poor beast's huge ears. She scuffled and fought the frightened animal to lead it into the inn. All the while the lead muleteer screamed at her. Once the mules in the train smelled the hay and water, though, they clomped to the stalls to eagerly eat and drink. But Jeannie and Gladys still had to deal with the angry lead muleteer.

Chi-la fan ma? asked Yang, just at the right time.

Yang—holding the most appetizing food he had ever

prepared—escorted the muleteers to the room where they were to eat. Gladys, of course, knew every way of making people feel comfortable. How she pampered the guests! Yang told stories to their first guests. His story made Jeannie's eyes open wide with concern. It was the next day that Jeannie repeated to Gladys Yang's version of how Noah filled the ark with animals and sailed safely to the inn at Bethlehem.

"Still our own inn is now really born," Gladys reasoned.

CHAPTER 5

The three Christians in the Inn of the Eight Happinesses worked very hard. The news of their special hospitality spread. Soon they had half a dozen mule trains staying at the inn every night. Forty to fifty mules usually munched happily in the stalls. As many as one hundred muleteers and helpers slept contentedly in the three dormitories. Guests were now enough at ease that Jeannie could tell the stories in the evening. Meanwhile, in every spare moment Gladys practiced Chinese, even memorizing Bible stories in Chinese. She had to master the language so she could spread the gospel, too. Also, Jeannie's illness grew worse.

I must go out among the people and learn to survive among them, Gladys realized.

So Gladys ventured out. She was struck by the appearance of Chinese women. They shuffled when they walked. Gladys was horrified to discover that their feet were bound so that the toes curled under. Yet these poor women scoffed that the foreign ladies' feet were about as elegant as elephant feet. Because Gladys wore a size three shoe, she was able to see humor in that. The Chinese women thought the foreign ladies' hands just as gross, especially their thick stumps of fingers. Gladys looked at her tiny hands and fingers and had to laugh at that, too.

Some of their customs were quaint. For example, if two people met on a narrow path the one who stopped first was allowed the right of way. So anticipating such an encounter was second nature to them. Gladys was never able to be the first to stop. Always she had to step off the path—often into the mud or a snowdrift—to let the other person pass. Jeannie said that was the custom over all the parts of China she had seen. Such universal customs were amazing to Gladys, because except for the muleteers, most Chinese did very little traveling.

"Yes, everywhere I have gone I have observed that many customs are the same," marveled Jeannie.

Of course there was the fine art of "saving face." Contrary to what westerners thought this meant, a gracious person did everything possible to let the other person save face. If, for example, Yang found out a deliveryman had been overcharging him for yams, Yang would inform the man the two foreign ladies had told him he must cut back on the money he spent on yams. Thus warned, the shrewd man would continue to deliver the same number of yams but charge Yang less. If that didn't work, Yang would pass the word to one of the man's relatives. Soon enough, the deliveryman would change. Or he might appear one day to tell Yang he couldn't make deliveries to the inn anymore; he was moving on to bigger and better things.

As Gladys walked through Yangcheng, she saw Buddhist priests, heads shaved, wearing bright orange vestments. She also saw Taoist priests, robed in scarlet. Certainly Buddhism and Taoism seemed distinct religions. "Just how do the Chinese balance these beliefs?" she asked Jeannie.

"The common Chinese ignore Buddhist priests with as much indifference as they would ignore a college professor. The Taoist priests are really men trained in rituals and completely uneducated in Taoism. The common Chinese are not really very religious at all. Even though the poorest of the poor observe rituals, they honor them more from custom than religion. The real root of their beliefs is a simple form of Confucianism."

It was a good thing Gladys had ventured forth and started to know Yangcheng, because Jeannie began to fail. After Gladys had been there for over a year, Jeannie disappeared one day. It was some time later before Gladys was able to find her in the remote village of Chin Shui. Jeannie had stormed into an inn there, perhaps thinking it was her own. She had fallen over a balcony. She landed on the pile of coal. She was very badly injured. Yet she lived—sometimes coherent and sometimes not—day after day.

"Take me home," she asked Gladys in her coherent moments.

After several weeks they were able to return to Yangcheng. The sight of Yangcheng filled Gladys with joy. Yang had kept the faith for all those weeks. He still ran the inn, possibly because it allowed him to regale muleteers and their helpers with stories of Noah, of whom he was extremely fond. Jeannie had called this place "home." Now for the first time, Gladys also felt this very wonderful place was her home, too. Yes, she loved Yangcheng and these innocent people. Even if Jeannie died, Gladys must somehow remain.

The Chinese kept coffins in their houses. Coffins were possessions of pride for them. "See how well I've provided for myself," they seemed to say. Even this custom seemed quaint to Gladys now, not morbid as she once thought. Jeannie's own coffin of shiny black wood stood upright near her bed. It gave her comfort, although she was virtually mute now. *Jeannie has become almost completely Chinese,* thought Gladys.

But what am I thinking? realized Gladys with a start. *It is the good news of the gospel that must comfort Jeannie. The coffin is only a resting place, temporary at that, for her worn-out shell. Her soul will be with God.* And she read from the Bible to Jeannie.

On December 1, 1931, Jeannie Lawson died.

Before the procession to the cemetery, the coffin—with Jeannie inside—was placed in front of the inn in the bright sunshine. A banner proclaiming Jeannie's goodness ran the length of the black coffin. Flowers also adorned it. Yang arranged for a photographer. Gladys sat beside the coffin, stunned to see how many Chinese flocked to get into the photograph beside her, behind her, and in front of her. The image of Jeannie and Gladys as foreign devils had truly ended. Over thirty people, toddlers to bearded sages, wanted this honor.

"And will you look at me?" gasped Gladys as she looked at the photograph later.

Sober-faced Gladys, in silk coat and trousers, hands clasped, was almost indistinguishable from the sober-faced Chinese ladies around her! Her long stay with Jeannie among the mountain people in Chin Shui had sharpened her understanding of the Chinese language, too. She was very comfortable now with her task. Now she, too, told Bible stories in the large room illuminated by several castor-oil lamps.

"Perhaps you should visit the Mandarin and pay your respects," said Yang out of the blue one day.

"The Mandarin?" answered a surprised Gladys.

Why had no one ever mentioned visiting this local ruler before? Was it because poor Jeannie's unpredictable moods had made it too risky? Whatever the reason, Yang was not one to be frivolous. Gladys began to suspect some kind of face-saving going on here. Was the Mandarin curious about her? Had emissaries of the Mandarin put the idea into Yang's head? How was she supposed to behave before the Mandarin? Gladys was confused. So she did nothing.

Just a few days later Yang burst into the inn. "The Mandarin is coming! The Mandarin is coming! You must go to the front door!"

Gladys felt very self-conscious but went to the front door. "Welcome to the Inn of Eight Happinesses," she said, bowing.

Through the front door paraded men in blue robes, some young and some graybeards. Finally, in came a bright red and black sedan chair carried by nervous-looking servants. The windows of the chair were curtained. The sedan chair was placed down in the exact center of the courtyard. One servant opened the door to the chair, almost bent double, yet offering his arm to the passenger in the chair.

"One dares not make a mistake in front of the Mandarin," gulped Gladys under her breath.

A tall man stepped out. He was as distinct from the others as a ruby among rough chunks of coal. He was a calm in the storm. His high-necked, wide-sleeved robe was brilliant red silk. His mustache dropped down at the corners. He wore a red skullcap. A long braid went down his back. He slowly turned, as if taking in the totality of the inn. When his eyes spotted Gladys, who still stood open-mouthed and gawking at the front door, she realized she was being rude. She bent double so fast she almost tumbled over on her face. She could hear him and his attendants approaching her.

"Counsel on a certain subject would be helpful," said a voice in very crisp, precise Chinese.

"A certain subject, Your Eminence?" she blurted nervously, not sure who was speaking to whom. Did she dare look at the Mandarin?

"You may rise, foreign lady," said the crisp voice again.

Gladys stood straight, still lowering her eyes. She must take the greatest care. There was no humor, no warmth in this voice, only extreme refinement. Yes, it was the Mandarin speaking. The brilliant red silk robe stood directly in front of her.

"For thousands of years," the voice said distinctly, "the

feet of females have been bound since infancy."

"Yes, Your Eminence," replied Gladys.

"The national government has decreed foot-binding illegal," said the Mandarin, with a tinge of irritation.

"Yes, Your Eminence," repeated Gladys. What had any of this to do with her?

"I am to stop the practice of foot-binding as quickly as possible," emphasized the Mandarin. "My jurisdiction includes many surrounding villages, as well as Yangcheng. Someone representing me must go to all these places to inform the people of this new decree. But more is required. A woman must go to inspect and unbind all feet. To show it is not unknown for a woman to have such feet, the woman should have unbound feet herself. Perhaps you know of such a woman?"

Then the Mandarin departed. Gladys had worked in service to the rich for many years. She knew an indirect order when she heard it. But she didn't want to be a foot inspector. What would become of the inn? But a very nervous Yang told her their local Mandarin answered only to the great warlord of all Shansi. In his own district, the Mandarin wielded the power of life and death over everyone. Gladys knew Yang wanted to scream, "If you don't do what the Mandarin says, we will all die!"

A few days later the Mandarin returned. "Have you found a woman to inspect foot-binding in my district?" he asked bluntly.

"Your Eminence, I wanted to make sure you had the

very best foot inspector possible, so I have written many letters. . . ."

"An excellent start," the Mandarin purred. "In the meantime, I am sure you will want to assume the duty yourself."

"Yes, Your Eminence," said Gladys, bowing deeply. She felt shamed. Then her heart filled with courage. She took a deep breath and said, "But while I am in these villages I will speak to the people about Jesus Christ."

"You may speak of your philosophy if you wish," he said coldly. His tone implied her religion worried him not in the slightest. "The guards and the mules will arrive here tomorrow morning at dawn. I expect you will be starting your inspections immediately."

"Gladly, Your Eminence."

Thus Gladys became a "foot inspector" for the Mandarin.

CHAPTER 6

When Gladys reflected on her new job as foot inspector, she realized it was truly a gift from God. She had the opportunity to travel all over the Mandarin's district and meet every woman and girl of the many thousands in the district. It really was miraculous. Why had she ever hesitated?

Here is yet another way to spread the gospel, she realized. *And to women.*

The next morning two guards arrived in the courtyard for Gladys. They bowed before her. Gladys bowed back. They insisted on loading her small bag with a writing tablet and other supplies on one of their two mules. They helped her into the saddle of the other mule. It was obvious the Mandarin had instructed them to take good care of his foot inspector for the district.

"Good-bye, honorable Miss Aylward," called Yang.

Gladys was amazed to see Yang locked in a deep bow. Apparently she was someone who commanded respect now. She and the guards plodded off to begin the foot inspections. The initial step was to inform the neighborhood elders and make sure they understood the decree was from the Mandarin. When she returned at a specified time, usually one day later, every woman and girl was supposed to be waiting at a specified place. The first time she returned to a neighborhood to the appointed place at the appointed time she understood the strength of the Mandarin's authority. A mob of females fidgeted while they waited for her. They were frightened, too.

"Bring your baby to me," Gladys told the first woman in line with an infant. Standing on a box so everyone could see her, Gladys unbound the tiny feet with great ceremony and massaged the baby's toes. "Now she will have strong, healthy feet!" yelled Gladys with authority. *How! How! How!* she added, which meant, "Good! Good! Good!"

Toddlers could express their delight after being unbound. Soon after Gladys gently massaged their toes back to normal, they sprang and jumped for joy. It was in the older girls that the depth of this cruel custom struck Gladys. Feet of girls beyond about ten years old seemed beyond rehabilitation. All Gladys could do was to urge them to no longer bind their feet and to encourage them to try to gradually uncramp the hideously deformed feet. Perhaps the bones of their feet still had enough youth in them to become almost normal someday.

"Forgive me, God," prayed Gladys, "for ever thinking this task was an indignity below my station."

It was many weeks before Gladys actually went off to the outlying villages. By that time, her visits were not a surprise. The word had spread. But the gospel was a surprise. For Gladys Aylward was now bringing the good news of Jesus Christ to these remote mountains. Was it possible that only two years before she had worked as a parlor maid in an English mansion? For it seemed now to Gladys that no other world existed except this bright, mountainous world of Shansi.

However, on one of her returns to Yangcheng a messenger stormed into the inn. "Come right away," he wailed. "There's a riot at the jail!"

"What does that have to do with me?" asked Gladys.

"Come right away. It's an official order." He flapped a piece of red paper wildly.

Gladys shrugged and proceeded to the jail. She was not prepared for what she heard as she approached the jail. Screams of rebellion! Or were they screams of chaos? The warden of the jail was waiting for her.

"You must go in and stop the fighting among the prisoners," he blurted to Gladys.

"But why me?" gasped Gladys in exasperation.

"They tell me you preach everywhere that your God is a living God Who protects you," said the warden.

"Yes, but. . ."

"Well, is your God all powerful or not? Do you really believe what you preach or not?" he plied.

A crowd gathered around the jail now because of the commotion. Gladys and her Christianity were on trial. Had the warden truly wanted her help out of desperation? Or had he slyly figured out that this misfortune could be used in a way to expose the foreign devil's Christianity as a fraud? Gladys was angry inside for being maneuvered into such a scary situation. *Oh, please, God,* she prayed, *give me courage and wisdom.*

"I will go into the jail," she announced loudly. "But only through the help of Jesus Christ will I prevail! For our Bible says, " 'I can do all things through Christ which strengtheneth me.' "

"Faith. Faith. Faith." She chanted this word each step she took to walk inside the walls of the jail and then through a passageway to the courtyard. By the time she reached a massive gate in the passageway that ran into the main courtyard, she was calm. Hysterical screams came from inside. The one jail guard at the massive gate looked rattled.

Gladys said, "Open the gate."

The guard opened the gate. She took a deep breath and walked through the gate. The gate clanged shut behind her. She forced herself to walk the rest of the way to the opening into the courtyard. There she stopped, numbed at the sight. The prisoners had not seen her. She seemed to be floating, free for the time being to take in the sight of the battle. The courtyard square was about sixty feet on a side, each side a wall of barred cells. The prisoners, perhaps fifty in all, were in a state of total hostility to each other, every one poised to spring any direction, intensely alert to react to each other's movements. Each occupied a tiny territory about ten feet square. Whatever had already happened had resulted in several prisoners lying in the dirt. Some may have been beaten unconscious. Some had crimson wounds.

"Ah, there is the center of the fight," Gladys observed.

One man clutched a huge meat knife, ready to strike. No

one else had such a weapon, as far as Gladys could tell. The man with the knife threatened his neighbor with his deadly weapon. His intended victim darted away, warily watching all his neighbors, too. The man with the knife seemed to be eyeing potential victims. But suddenly the atmosphere changed.

Lao-yang-kwei! she heard someone yell.

One pair of eyes after another turned to the "foreign devil" —Gladys. Suddenly the man with the knife was not ten feet away, glowering at her. It was now she had to act.

She stepped toward him. "Hand that knife to me!" she commanded.

His face seemed to almost explode as he hesitated. Should he strike this foreign devil? Suddenly his face dissolved into meekness. He handed her the knife.

"Now, all of you stop shouting," she barked. "Form ranks in front of me!"

They formed ranks. Half a dozen remained on the ground. Several crept out of cells they had been hiding in. The danger over, Gladys now digested the fact that these prisoners were the most pitiful people she had ever seen. They had sunk far below poverty. Their clothing seemed nothing but tattered rags. They were bone thin. Their shaved heads exposed scabs. Gladys knew they were crawling with lice. They smelled of vomit and worse. Gladys wanted to cry with pity, but she must keep them under control.

"Do you have no shame?" she scolded. "Look at you. A flock of chickens has more dignity."

"We have no purpose. . . ," mumbled a man in the front row.

"Oh, stop feeling sorry for yourself! Appoint a spokesman. I will talk to him while the rest of you clean up this mess. Perhaps then the warden will be in a better mood when he hands out punishment."

While the prisoners cleaned the courtyard and tended the wounded, Gladys spoke to their spokesman, a prisoner named Feng. Feng knew only that the fight started over the knife itself. The prisoners were allowed to use it for an hour or so to cut up food. Perhaps someone used it too long. Perhaps someone took it out of turn. Who could know now? Food was a matter that preyed on every prisoner's mind constantly. The jail itself supplied no food. Food was supplied only by relatives or friends. Some men were starving.

"What do you do during the day?" asked Gladys.

"Nothing," answered Feng hollowly. "We wait for time to pass. Occasionally, one of us is removed to be executed. Occasionally, one of us dies from something else. They chain a gang of us together to take the dead man down the mountainside at night and bury him."

Gladys went outside and drew the warden aside. "I am sure the Mandarin would be pleased to learn the fighting not only stopped but it inspired you to improve the conditions of the jail."

"Improve the jail?"

"You must give these men work."

"You are foreign. You do not understand. We have very strict labor guilds in Shansi that prevent unauthorized work. The Mandarin himself presides over the allotments!"

"There must be some work they can do. Don't you see that if they could earn a little money they could buy food for themselves? Maybe even clothing. Straw for their cells. If you suggest this to the Mandarin, then he can decide what kind of work might be available."

"This is very unusual," mulled the warden.

"Perhaps I could make the suggestion to the Mandarin," said Gladys slyly.

"No!" blurted the warden.

"One more thing." Gladys saw the warden cringe. He expected her to gloat over her triumph in the courtyard. Her God was indeed all powerful. But Gladys only said, "I promised the prisoners you would be lenient. I wish no one to be severely punished for this incident."

His face fell. "But some men might die from their wounds."

"Go ahead and punish them as you wish, then. But when you have your next problem here, you cannot send for me. They would have no faith in me a second time."

He blinked. "I'll do what you suggest."

Gladys waited patiently for the warden to handle the affair with the Mandarin. Meanwhile she regularly visited the jail. She brought them the good news of Jesus Christ. She encouraged cleanliness. She had to bolster the prisoners until some kind of reform could begin. The Mandarin did find work for them that no one else wanted to do. It wasn't long before the prisoners had two old looms making coarse cotton fabric, some of which they used to make their own shoes. The rest they used to make the ankle wraps that secured the bottoms of trousers. The ankle wraps they were allowed to sell. They also ground corn for money.

Although Gladys wanted no credit for herself for stopping the riot, the rumor spread that it was the tiny foreign lady who had performed the miracle. The warden had challenged her living God in front of many witnesses. Now only a fool would not know this tiny woman was an *Ai-Weh-Deh*.

Chi-la fan ma, Ai-Weh-Deh! seemed to echo from every doorway now when Gladys passed.

Ai-Weh-Deh meant "Virtuous One."

CHAPTER 7

It was 1933.

Gladys marveled at how her ministry was growing. She preached to the passing mule trains. Because of her job as foot inspector, she preached in Yangcheng and other villages. And now she also preached in jails all over her district. One day she was in Yangcheng, walking to report to the Mandarin on her trip as foot inspector to one of the outer villages. She stopped abruptly. A woman and a child sat against a wall. The woman's face was dirty and oily from neglect. Her hair was plastered down. Her clothing was the common high-necked tunic over baggy pants, but it was filthy. Yet the woman was immaculate compared to the child slumped against her. The child wore only a very soiled loincloth. Sores covered the face and head. The belly was swollen.

"That child looks very sick," said Gladys.

"Do you want to buy this child or not?" snarled the woman.

"Now I see what you're doing!" snapped Gladys.

"The price is cheap. Two silver dollars."

Gladys was ready to explode. The woman was one of the evil child sellers she had heard about. Gladys continued on. This was definitely something she should tell the Mandarin about. She bowed as she entered his presence. Many courtesies always had to be observed first. This time they only aggravated her as she waited for a chance to speak things of substance. The unbinding of the women's feet in the villages was proceeding very well, she assured him. She agonized over whether or not to protest the selling of children. Yet God gave her no choice.

She blurted, "There is a woman very near here trying to sell a child."

"Don't interfere, *Ai-Weh-Deh*," he cautioned. "Selling children is wicked, but if you interfere with the woman she is likely to do something far worse to the child, especially if it's a girl. . . ."

"I came to China to answer the call from Jesus Christ," Gladys said hotly. "I will not respect customs that are an insult to His love!"

She exited rapidly. She felt sick. How would the Mandarin take this disrespect? At least no one else had been present. Perhaps he would forgive her. She certainly would not drop the matter. She would see just how far she could push the woman. Gladys had only ninepence in coppers in her pocket. If it was God's will, she would be able to save the child with that paltry sum.

Gladys snapped at the woman, "I don't have two dollars."

"One dollar then," grumbled the woman bitterly.

After much angry haggling—and finally what seemed a miracle to Gladys—she walked back to the Inn of Eight Happinesses penniless but carrying a very sick child. Perhaps the woman had thought the child was so close to dying she might not ever get any money at all for the poor thing.

Yang was astonished. "This child is almost dead." His tone carried a reprimand.

"Get a bowl of cereal."

Yang returned to place the bowl down near the child. The skinny limbs of the toddler sprang to life to snatch the bowl, then to run off into a corner to eat. Only when she was able to clean the child did Gladys realize it was a girl. Gladys affectionately called the girl "Ninepence." They learned she was not three or four years of age but a very undernourished six. Gladys tried to find a home for the girl. But that was not possible.

"So God has decided she stays here," said Gladys to Yang. "Ninepence is all right as a nickname, but I'm going to christen her Mei-en."

" 'Beautiful Grace' is a very good name," agreed Yang.

But the firestorm over Ninepence had involved the Mandarin, too. Gladys had been very abrupt with him, very rude. The next time she went to report to him about a foot inspection she was worried. He was far too disciplined to show his disapproval before the usual courtesies.

But finally, his face unreadable, the Mandarin said, "They tell me you purchased that child on the street."

"Mei-en is my daughter now, Eminence," replied Gladys.

"They tell me she was as wild as a wolf for awhile."

"It was the ferocity of God bringing her back to life."

"Perhaps. . ." He paused.

She excused herself. She had learned to do that when he paused for awhile. It was her signal to leave. But the Mandarin had made no complaint about her disobedience. In fact, in his own cool way he seemed friendlier than ever before. Ninepence was definitely a gift from God.

One day Ninepence—by then healthy and strong—came to her at dinnertime. "If I ate less of the meal, could you also eat less of it?"

"Less, less, less. What are you up to?"

"There is a boy at the gate who has nothing to eat. We can give him our two 'lesses.' "

The boy was about eight, dressed in ragged clothes, not nearly warm enough for winter. He was from a tiny village far east of Yangcheng. Bandits had raided his village and killed his father. His mother took him and fled. But she died on the trail. A mule train brought the boy into Yangcheng where he begged on the streets. He was open-faced, with not a trace of self-pity. He was so brave and his story was so sad it tore at Gladys's heart.

"You will stay with us from now on," she told the boy.

Inspired by Ninepence's introduction, Gladys nicknamed the boy "Less." One day the following spring Ninepence and Less appeared with a toddler in tow. This child was about two years old, with that blinking, bewildered look worn by abandoned innocents. Gladys had the town crier broadcast the boy's dilemma. No one claimed him. He became the third child Gladys took in. He became "Bao Bao," her "Precious

Bundle." And Gladys took in more and more children.

One day when Gladys gave her report to the Mandarin, he never paused to indicate to her the audience was over. This time he kept the conversation going. They discussed many topics. He was very curious about Christianity. But he later shocked Gladys with news about what was happening in China.

"Do you not know Japan has invaded our eastern territories? They won't be satisfied with just that much. Then there are our own Chinese Communists—as vicious a pack of wolves who ever roamed the Chinese wilderness—biding their time far to our south."

But the troubles all seemed very far away to Gladys. In 1936, she became a citizen of China. No one had better call her a foreign devil anymore. Other missionaries told her now that she knew the mountain dialects better than any other missionary. Gladys was saddened by Mrs. Smith's death in Tsechow. Mrs. Smith was replaced by David and Jean Davis, who were almost the same age as Gladys. David Davis was also very concerned about the Japanese and the Communists. But Gladys did not feel threatened. Even in July 1937 when fighting broke out between Chinese and Japanese near Beijing, it seemed very far away.

One spring morning of 1938, Gladys was kneeling in prayer in an upstairs room at the Inn of Eight Happinesses. Yang was with her, as well as four other Christian converts.

"I hear a peculiar buzzing noise!" said Yang, embarrassed

that he had to interrupt prayers.

Gladys listened hard. "It's getting louder." The windows were not papered now that it was spring. Gladys rose to walk to an open window. The street below swarmed with people. Everyone was looking up at the sky. "What do you see?" she yelled down.

"Beautiful silver birds, *Ai-Weh-Deh!*" Their faces were beaming.

Suddenly there was an explosion that rattled her bones. Another. Another. Bombs! War had come to Yangcheng! The street below was lost in a flash. The world fell away. Every- thing was black. Sometime later, Gladys heard the murmur of voices. There were no explosions now, only weight crushing her back.

"They're under here!" screamed a voice.

Finally the weight was off her back. Hands were turning her. She blinked at blue sky. The roof was gone! Anxious faces ogled her. She was lifted and carried somewhere. Gradually she regained her senses. All who had been in the room with her were alive, too. A bomb had struck the corner of the inn. Nine people out on the street had died. Gladys and the others had tumbled out of the disintegrating room to fall on other rubble below. Then they were covered by more cascading rubble. Gladys had been unconscious for some time.

"Help me up," she said.

She was shaken, bruised, and scratched, but otherwise seemed all right. She walked on wobbly legs to get her medicine kit. She had little more than wads of cotton, a can of borax powder for cleaning wounds, and a bottle of permanganate of potash for a disinfectant, but it would do. She had Yang tear sheets in strips for bandaging. Then they went inside the wall at the East Gate to the main street of Yangcheng. Piles of rubble testified to the devastation. Many people were dead. Wounded people were groaning, some in sight, some covered by debris.

"We have no time to mourn," snapped Gladys.

She organized a brigade.

CHAPTER 8

All day long, Gladys and her brigade worked their way down the main street of Yangcheng. Strong young men uncovered the bodies. They carried the dead outside the city walls to be buried later. They carried the wounded inside any buildings still standing. There Gladys and the women attended the wounds. They were able to clean a wound, disinfect it, and bandage it. But stitching and setting of broken bones had to wait for more skilled medical hands.

By late afternoon, the Mandarin and his officials received terrifying news. Japanese foot soldiers were only sixty miles away. The Mandarin decided they must take no more than a day or two to bury their dead. Then they had to go off with the wounded to villages in the remotest parts of the mountains. Gladys and many of her Christian converts, about forty in all, would trek to Bei Chai Chuang. But Yang had decided to return to his home village. Tears blinded Gladys as she said farewell to him.

"Praise God my children are all alive and with me," she consoled herself as they finally trudged off to Bei Chai Chuang.

There was not even a trail to Bei Chai Chung. Yet, as tiny and remote as it was, it was within walls. Just eight houses. As foot inspector, Gladys had been at Bei Chai Chuang before. The people there welcomed Gladys and the refugees without hesitation. The life the villagers led was simple but sufficient. They farmed tiny plots of millet, corn, and cotton. They tended pigs, sheep, cattle, and chickens. They trapped pheasants and rabbits.

In the days ahead, the refugees walked to the crest of the mountain to see silvery Japanese planes cruising the valleys below. Once Gladys ventured alone back to Yangcheng. But she was almost trapped in a battle between khaki-uniformed Japanese soldiers and blue-uniformed Chinese soldiers. She barely escaped. As she climbed once again toward Bei Chai Chuang, she spotted an entire Japanese army marching through a canyon toward Yangcheng. Yet only days later she heard the Japanese abandoned Yangcheng. They did not want to be over-extended when winter came. But Gladys knew they would return.

Reliable sources told her the Japanese were merciless. She no longer regarded Bei Chai Chuang as some temporary stopover. Many mountain people lived in caves dug into the mountainside. That was the destiny of Gladys and her large group. They carefully sculpted the inside of their cave into a large arched room and built supports. They walled off the opening with stone. Because Gladys had medical supplies, word spread among the mountain people that a "hospital" existed in Bei Chai Chuang. Wounded Chinese straggled in.

"Welcome, friend," Gladys would say without fail, then begin her limited medical treatment.

Of course, her job as foot inspector was suspended

indefinitely, but she still visited villages to tend to her Christian converts. Yangcheng and her inn were in ruins. Restoration seemed futile. Even the age-old mule trains had stopped. No one looked forward to spring. Springtime would bring the Japanese war machine again. But that winter brought a great surprise when she visited Yangcheng. The Mandarin had debated with her the merits of her faith against the merits of his Confucius ways many times.

"But Confucianism lives in my head," he declared, "not in my heart, as Christianity does in *Ai-Weh-Deh* and her converts." Then he concluded, "I, too, wish to become a Christian!"

He told Gladys that more than anyone he had ever met she demonstrated the power of love. Before she departed to Bei Chai Chuang, she instructed the Mandarin as a new Christian. After returning to Bei Chai Chuang, she was compelled that spring to go to Chin Shui to her small mission there. Japanese dive-bombers were raining bombs on the village as she approached. Then the wings of death departed. She quickly organized her charges, telling them where to find refuge higher in the mountains. Approaching Japanese foot soldiers fired upon them as they fled.

By February 1939, she became so concerned about David Davis and his mission that she slipped down into Tsechow. Japanese occupied Tsechow, but she did not have to take the risk of entering the well-guarded gates of the city. The mission, like her own in Yangcheng, lay outside the city walls. Davis and his wife Jean welcomed Gladys. But one night Gladys awakened to shouts and screams. She burst out of her room. The courtyard swarmed with Japanese soldiers. Their voices were loud, rasping, full of stupidity. They were drunk. They wanted women.

"Get out of here, you devils!" screamed Gladys.

A soldier slammed his rifle butt into the side of her head. The next thing Gladys knew, Jean Davis was staring into her face with great concern. Slowly Gladys regained her senses. The women were safe, she was told. David Davis had arrived after Gladys had been knocked out. The women dragged into the courtyard by the drunken soldiers had all fallen to their knees at David's command. They all started loudly praying. Somehow God made the terrible shame of what the Japanese soldiers were about to do sink into their drunken consciences. Miraculously the soldiers departed. But David had paid a price.

"He is being stitched up by a doctor," said Jean.

Both Gladys and David Davis recovered. David left to take two elderly missionaries far south where they might still get passage back to England. He would be gone many weeks. Then the Japanese abruptly retreated from Tsechow. Winter once again belonged to the Chinese soldiers. That was when Gladys met Colonel Linnan of the Intelligence Service. He was as quiet-spoken and well-mannered as the Mandarin.

"I am a Chinese citizen, too," Gladys told him.

"You are Chinese!" He seemed delighted.

If only she knew how difficult it was to accomplish change in China, he said. Their leader Chiang Kai-shek was a very good man, a frugal, faithful man, he insisted. Chiang was a Christian married to a Christian wife. Many improvements had not been made by his Nationalist government, but it was not because Chiang Kai-shek did not want to make the improvements. It was because the old warlords resisted the changes. And then just when Chiang Kai-shek seemed to be making real progress, the Japanese had invaded. Gladys was very impressed by Colonel Linnan. He began to visit her frequently. She even strolled with him inside the city. She wrote her parents a letter, preparing them for the possibility of her marriage to a Chinese colonel. And just before she left for the mountains, he treated her to a very worried look.

"I won't be able to relax until you return," he said.

He makes my heart sing, she admitted to herself as she went up into the mountains.

Colonel Linnan was certainly present in her heart now. Never had Gladys felt so bonded to China. She agonized, too. Just how much could she as a Christian do for China? Surely she was justified in helping refugees flee Japanese tyranny. But could she do more? This dilemma arose once more when she again saw Colonel Linnan.

"I often see Japanese troops when I travel," she said.

"So dangerous!" he objected.

"They never bother me. I guess I look very harmless."

"They truly take no note of you?" Colonel Linnan's mind

was racing. "It would be most helpful to China if we knew the locations of any of their advance scouting parties. Or any troop movements."

When he next returned, he had a letter he wanted Gladys to carry. It was official permission from the Chinese government for Gladys to "scout." So she did. If she saw Japanese troops, she informed the nearest Chinese soldiers. War seemed a never-ending nightmare for Gladys. How many years had this insanity been going on? Once again in a flood of refugees running toward the remote mountains—this time from Lingchuang—she was fired upon by foot soldiers. Japanese warplanes rained bullets into them, too. Hundreds of innocents died. Gladys and other surviving refugees scrambled off into the mountains.

The war worsened. Gladys became obsessed with the two hundred orphans at the Davis mission outside Tsechow. Her own precious children were there, too. Something had to be done before the next great spring offensive by the Japanese. How many chances to escape death would these two hundred young charges get? Then she heard that if the orphans could be brought to Sian, far west of the Japanese threat, they would be cared for. Someone had to walk them south to the Yellow River. There they could be ferried across the vast river. Then a train would take them west to Sian. But they must accomplish it before the Japanese returned. In early 1940, one of the mission helpers—a strong young man—left Tsechow with half the orphan children. Many weeks later, Gladys learned the children reached Sian safely. But then she learned the helper had been captured by the Japanese trying to return to Tsechow. What would become of the one hundred children still remaining in Tsechow? For she had just heard the Japanese had started their spring attack.

After much prayer Gladys told David Davis, who had returned to Tsechow, "I must take the remaining one hundred orphans to Sian myself. . . ."

"First I will move all the orphans to the inn at Yangcheng," Gladys told Davis. "The Japanese never take Yangcheng until after they take Tsechow."

So her helpers shepherded the children up the heights to the now ramshackle Inn of Eight Happinesses at Yangcheng. Gladys remained in Tsechow. Nearly one thousand other refugees were still at the mission. She helped David Davis arrange their plans of flight. But one afternoon Davis told her the Japanese were one day away from Tsechow. Gladys must leave. Later one of the helpers approached her.

"There is a price on your head now," he said.

"I can't believe it," she objected.

"Read this," he said, handing her a notice the Japanese were posting here and there.

Gladys read the handbill. Yes, there was a reward for the Mandarin. But there was also a reward for "the small woman known as *Ai-Weh-Deh*." She was called a spy! Gladys was numb with dread. The handbill was her death warrant. Had she waited too long? She had to get to Yangcheng. She gathered her few belongings. Before she left, she burned her correspondence. Included in the flames was a letter from her parents saying it was fine with them if she wanted to marry the Chinese colonel.

"The Japanese are entering the city!" screamed someone.

The mission lay outside the city walls. Gladys dashed out the back gate of the mission into a cemetery. To her horror, she saw a long line of marching soldiers only one hundred yards away. Bullets sang past her. An old ditch lay ahead of her. If only she could reach it. Something whomped her in the back. The next thing she knew she was flat on her face. Clutching her bundle, she crawled into the ditch, bullets whining all around her. Her fingers probed a stinging area of her right shoulder. There was very little blood. A bullet must have just grazed her. Then miraculously the soldiers disregarded her. They had more important prey to press. Still, she waited until dark to begin the journey to Yangcheng. There, two days later, she told the Mandarin she was fleeing Shansi.

"How much food do you have?" he asked.

"Whatever you give us, Eminence."

"Us?"

"I'm taking the orphans with me."

"But aren't there several dozen, *Ai-Weh-Deh?*"

"About one hundred."

Gladys left, knowing that the Mandarin had a price on his head, too. She might be able to flee Shansi. But he could not leave his district. During all the ebb and flow of these battles he must never be caught, because he would be executed. So why should she think her trek with the children was such an impossible task?

"Tomorrow we are going for a long walk in the mountains," she told the excited orphans at the inn. "At dawn you will roll your chopsticks and bowls up inside your bedding. Get a good night's sleep."

Although Gladys chose to avoid established trails, the first part of their trek was not difficult for these children. It spoke of the harsh reality of China that the seventy children aged four to eight had taken many hard journeys. So, of course, had the boys and girls older than eight. For lunch the caravan stopped by a stream to boil some millet. That evening the children slept in a remote Buddhist temple. The next night they were not so lucky. They huddled under their quilts in the cold mountain night. The third night was in a village.

"How many days will it take to reach the Yellow River?" Ninepence asked Gladys discreetly.

"The mule trains take only five days to make the journey," answered Gladys.

But mules walked much faster and steadier than four year olds. And the mule trains used the main trail. Gladys had to avoid the main trail. Day after day the caravan of chattering urchins trudged to the southwest. Toward the end of the day, the older boys often carried the youngest ones on their backs. Where did they find such strength in their small bowls of millet? The oldest girls were the most helpless of all. Their feet, once bound, were weak and crippled. Gladys could scarcely keep from crying when she examined her entourage. After several days on the trek, the band of children was losing heart. Their feet were sore. They were underfed. They were very tired and cranky. Their clothes and bedding were torn and filthy. Their shoes were nearly worthless rags.

"Soldiers ahead!" yelled one of the older boys sent ahead by Gladys to scout.

Gladys crept forward. She peered down at a line of soldiers. One moment of supreme dread passed into a moment of great joy. Soon the children were frolicking among fifty Chinese soldiers, who treated them with food. The men were well supplied. They even had candy. Candy was almost unknown to these orphans. The soldiers departed the next morning. In a short time the children were all miserable again. Many had lost their bowls and chopsticks. Many were now barefoot. Their clothing and bedding reeked. They had been on the trek twelve days.

"The Yellow River!" screamed a scout.

There it was below them, vast and silvery from these heights. The troop of urchins scrambled down to the Yellow River. There was no trail, but no one minded now. A few hours later they trudged into a village called Yuan Ku. Only an old man was there. He told Gladys the Japanese now controlled this north side of the Yellow River. There was no longer a ferry across the river!

"No way to get across the river?" Gladys mumbled numbly.

She and the orphans camped by the river. The older boys foraged for food in the abandoned village. Gladys prayed. The days dragged by. On the fourth day Chinese soldiers appeared. They were a patrol of eight. The soldier in command of the patrol signaled someone on the other side of the river with a mirror. Brilliance flashed back from the other side.

"It will take three trips to get all of you across," he said, his eyes scouring the sky. "Enemy planes are usually very bad along this river."

But the crossing across the treacherous Yellow River was successful. Two days later, Gladys and the children were in Mien Chih, south of the river. Friendly villagers fed them, bathed them, and escorted them to the train station the next morning. Trains carried only refugees now. The children buzzed with excitement. Not one had ever seen a train before. When the train actually arrived, they were aghast. What a smoke-pluming, steam-spewing dragon it was! Everything about a train was loud. Clanging. Wrenching. Hissing. Screeching. Weren't things being devoured by this monster? The smallest children had to be coaxed aboard.

"Watch out for splinters!" yelled Gladys.

The cars were barren wooden boxcars. The children sprawled everywhere. After the train began click-click-clicking along the track, they were no longer frightened but calmed. The train wasn't so bad. And now they could rest their aching feet. They wiggled their toes and laughed. Occasionally the train would stop, and its passengers could get off and be fed at a refugee camp. But at a small village called Tiensan, Gladys was told the train would go no farther. A bridge had been destroyed by the Japanese. She resolved they would simply walk the track as she had done so many years ago in Russia. But no, that was not possible, she was warned. The Yellow River was very narrow there, and the Japanese could easily shoot them down from the other side. And they would.

"But we must get to Sian," she told her informant.

He gazed at the heights looming to the west. "Your only hope is to cross those mountains."

"What is the trail like?"

"I don't know. We never use the trail," he said weakly.

Gladys groaned inside. Those mountains looked more rugged than the ones in Shansi, and she didn't know these mountains. Many of the children were walking on rags now. *O God, give me wisdom,* she prayed. *What are we to do?* Yet somehow in the next days the bedraggled urchins climbed the mountain range and descended on the other side. Most were very sick. Gladys herself was having lapses of memory. Once in a village, they picked up the railroad again. Only coal trains ran. So the children climbed up into cars and sprawled on the hard coal. The train rumbled west to Sian. Finally they were there. Gladys was numbed to discover Sian a closed city. Sian would not take one more refugee. Then she learned the other orphans from Yangcheng were not in Sian, anyway. They had been diverted to Fufeng, eighty miles farther west. Gladys seemed lost in an endless journey. Nevertheless, she and her charges finally reached the orphanage in Fufeng.

"You look very sick to me," said a woman at the orphanage.

That was the last thing Gladys remembered for a very long time. . . .

CHAPTER 10

Even when she regained her consciousness later, she felt only half there. "Who are you?" she asked a white-clad woman. "Where am I?"

The startled woman answered, "Why, you're making sense for once!"

Soon a man hovered over Gladys. In English he said, "I say, the nurse tells me you've got your senses back. Jolly good show."

"Where am I? What happened?"

"I'm a senior physician at Baptist Hospital in Sian. You were brought here. You've babbled on and on for weeks. You had a severe fever. One hundred and five degrees. Your brain should have baked. You also had typhus. Pneumonia, as well. Yes, and malnutrition, too. Exhaustion. And a bullet seemed to have branded the back of your shoulder! Oh, well, good lady, I know now you're going to live."

"Are the children all right?"

"Children?"

"I have a hundred children. . . ."

Gladys was finally discharged. By now she knew she was considered a miracle at the hospital. Only the arrival of a new drug called sulphapyridine saved her from certain death. Apparently, she had helped in various ways with refugees for several months before collapsing. Gladys had no memory of an entire year. She found out many of her children were now in Sian, too, so she felt compelled to stay in the area around Fufeng and Sian. Gladys did not eat well. She did not get enough sleep, either. She still occasionally blacked out. She was now forty years old.

In 1943, Colonel Linnan found Gladys in the Sian area. But Gladys was almost burned out. Her feeling for Colonel Linnan was no longer the desire of a woman in love but the warmth of a friend. Besides, Colonel Linnan had an ambitious career. He admitted it. A wife who had her own mission among the dispossessed would only tear him apart. And if she gave up her mission, she would be torn apart. And he was not a Christian.

"So it's over," she admitted numbly.

The next years continued the exhaustion and confusion for Gladys. She began to drift from mission to mission. Once she discovered herself far south in China. Once she found herself in a leper colony. Everywhere she served the dispossessed. Much of her experience seemed a dream. In 1945, she heard the Japanese had lost the war. But now China was in a civil war. Chiang Kai-shek's Nationalists were now fighting the Communists. China was a continuing nightmare.

One day she numbly told fellow workers, "I just heard my boy Less was yanked out of school by the Communists and shot. He's not the only one of my boys who has died for Christ. And my girl Ninepence got married, but I don't know where she is. I don't know if she is alive or not."

It seemed all the news was bad. She heard Yang had died. What had happened to the Mandarin? Perhaps it was best she didn't know. The Communists were ruthlessly successful in the civil war. Russian Communists had leaped into the war against Japan in the final few days to capture large depots of weapons. These they turned over to the Chinese Communists. Well-armed and ever ready to promise peasant recruits the moon, the Communists grew in strength. The Nationalists under Chiang Kai-shek had a long history of broken promises. By 1947, except for a few Nationalist strongholds, the Communists controlled all of north China. Nationalist China was about to collapse. Gladys, too—after many years of exhaustion and bad news—appeared about to collapse.

By 1949, thousands were fleeing China. Gladys was a Chinese citizen, but she was warned that, as a Christian, she would be executed by the Communists. But God gave Gladys a great treat before she left China. She found Ninepence in Shanghai. Ninepence had a toddling son. Then, after nineteen years, Gladys found herself back in England. Her parents, her sister, Violet, and her brother, Lawrence, were all alive. But Gladys had trouble adjusting to her old home. She chattered Chinese at astonished English faces. She was uncontrollably sad. The deaths of so many of her beloved children and China's impending collapse to godless Communism had broken her.

The news from China was all bad. Chiang Kai-shek and his remaining army were exiled to the large island of Formosa.

Gladys realized with a start that if she ever went back to China, it was only the China on that island of Formosa that was open to her. She also realized that all the old Christian missionaries were gone from China—or in prison. And what of the Mandarin? She would probably never know. And what was the fate of Colonel Linnan? Was it any wonder she was sad? She prayed for strength.

Suddenly wonderful things began to happen. Her command of English returned. Her compulsion to preach returned. She began giving talks. She liked to say she had just been "a simple London parlor maid, homely, poor, and ignorant—but willing!" A newspaper journalist wrote about her service in China. One day another journalist, Alan Burgess, came to visit her on Cheddington Road after reading one of the newspaper articles. Burgess was writing and producing for the British Broadcasting Company a series on war heroes called "The Undefeated." War heroes? *How nice,* thought Gladys. But how could she help him? She didn't really know any war heroes herself. Well, they didn't have to be war heroes in the strictest military sense, suggested Burgess. Heroes of great courage.

"Perhaps David Davis. . ."

"What about yourself?" he asked. "Surely you must have had an adventure or two over there." But his face was shrouded in doubt.

"Me? I've done nothing the people who listen to the British Broadcasting Company would think interesting."

"Did you come into contact with Japanese?"

"Well, yes." It wouldn't be very forgiving if she told Alan Burgess she had been shot down in a field outside Tsechow. Bombed, too. In Yangcheng. Strafed by a warplane, too. Smashed in the head once with a rifle butt, too. "Some of the Japanese are very nice, you know," she offered.

"I see you led a rather sheltered life in China," he sighed. Still he pressed her. "Surely you must have witnessed some adventure there?"

She shrugged. "My fondest memory is taking some children to an orphanage in the area around Sian."

"Really?" he said, not bothering to hide his disappointment. "Children? To an orphanage?"

"Yes, it was across some mountains."

"Across the mountains?" He perked up. "Real mountains?"

"Yes, I think you would call them real mountains. The trip was made more difficult because we couldn't use any main trails. Oh, and we had to cross the Yellow River, too."

"Isn't that the terribly dangerous river that floods so often it's called 'China's Sorrow'?"

Alan Burgess grew more and more animated as Gladys recalled her adventure. Finally he looked numb. He mumbled, "No food. No money. Just you and one hundred children for one month of travel across mountains, across rivers, through Japanese patrols. Under Japanese dive-bombers. And you were sick with fever and typhus and pneumonia and malnutrition? Yes, Miss Aylward, I think the British Broadcasting Company might be able to use your story. . . ."

Alan Burgess went on to write a book about Gladys. He interviewed her for four months. Then he went away to write the book. She forgot about the book. She had far too much to do for the Lord. Then precious Mum died. How it jolted Gladys. Mum dead and Gladys herself now fifty! Gladys must get on with her work. She had been in England too long. By the time the book—*The Small Woman*—came out in 1957, Gladys had already booked passage to Hong Kong. She had little interest in the book. When some company called Twentieth Century Fox wanted to buy the movie rights, she signed them over to the company with scarcely a thought.

"Well, if you're so foolish as to pay good money for the story of a mousey little parlor maid. . ."

Gladys eventually made it to Formosa, where Chiang Kai-shek was in exile. Formosa was already a showcase of what all of China could have accomplished under Chiang Kai-shek's Nationalist rule. The Formosans of "Free China" were building roads and industry. All citizens were being taught to read and write. So Gladys immediately became a teacher of Mandarin. She found several of her children. She settled in Taipei, living in her simple way. Then orphans started coming to Gladys. She attracted orphans like a magnet. She was concerned. She was now well past fifty. Would she have the energy? Maybe she had her doubts, but God had no doubts.

Surely He is the One gravitating these orphans toward me, reasoned Gladys.

People began talking about the movie that had been made of her great mountain adventure during the war. It was called not *The Inn of Eight Happinesses* but *The Inn of the Sixth Happiness.* The beautiful Swedish movie star Ingrid Bergman portrayed Gladys. German actor Curt Jergens was Colonel Linnan. It was a very polished, very successful movie. But Gladys was unhappy with the movie. It was full of inaccuracies. And she felt it was condescending to the brave Chinese.

"Oh, that movie!" she would sputter if it was mentioned.

She almost had a nervous breakdown over the movie. Yet

in the end, the movie benefited the gospel. The movie kept her in demand as a speaker. She used the opportunity to preach. She raised money for her orphans. She toured America, Australia, and New Zealand. She just had to grin and bear it when celebrity-worshippers asked her if she knew Ingrid Bergman personally. In England she met Queen Elizabeth herself.

Gladys, of course, did not pass up that opportunity. "The orphans in Formosa need help," she said to the queen.

At sixty Gladys found a volunteer, Kathleen Langston-Smith, to help manage the orphanage. Gladys had suffered much from war and from missionary work. Many of her children from Shansi had died, so she often fought depression. But she struggled on. As she said, she was always willing to serve. In January 1970, Gladys Aylward, sixty-seven years old and totally used up from her service, joined the Lord. Forty years before, she had prayed, "Use me, God! Oh, please use me. . . ."

JIM ELLIOT

MISSIONARY MARTYR

by Susan Martins Miller

CHAPTER 1

Jim Elliot did not know where he was going. But he knew that he was going somewhere that God had planned for him.

He did not know when he would go. But he wanted to be ready when it was time to go.

Lots of students who start college do not know what kind of job they want to have when they finish going to school. They think they will have fun while they are in college, and then they can decide later what kind of job to get. But Jim was not like this. He knew what he wanted to do. He did not want an ordinary job in the United States. He was smart and could be anything he wanted to be—doctor, lawyer, pastor, or anything else. But he wanted to be only one thing. Someday, somewhere, he would be a missionary. Going to college was one way of getting ready for that occupation.

Such were Jim Elliot's thoughts when he started going to Wheaton College in 1945. But he had already started getting ready to be a missionary even when he was a little boy.

Jim grew up in the state of Oregon on the slope of a mountain called Mt. Tabor. His mother was a chiropractor and his father was a Bible teacher. His parents read the Bible to Jim and his brothers and sister every day, and every day his father prayed with him. The whole family went to church every week. Jim's mother believed that it was good even for babies to learn to worship God.

Mr. and Mrs. Elliot believed in hard work, obedience, and honesty, and they tried to teach their children these qualities. The children had chores that they had to do every day. Jim's jobs included feeding chickens, stoking the furnace, cleaning up the yard, and running errands. His friends were surprised at how many chores he had to do, but Jim did not seem to mind. He just figured out the best way to get the work done and did the best he could. Sometimes he even got his friends to help him with his work. Because he grew up in such a family, Jim was not afraid of hard work, whether it was physical work or mental work.

But Jim knew how to have fun, too. He liked to take two of his friends hunting and camping. The boys did not have any money for equipment, but that did not stop them. Jim looked in all the stores where they could buy used equipment until he found just what they needed. On their first hunting trip, they shot a duck. Unfortunately, it was someone's pet duck!

When he was in high school, Jim played on the football team and was in the school plays. Some of his teachers thought he had enough talent to be a professional actor, but Jim was not interested in that. He liked being in the plays while he was young, but being an actor was not as interesting as being a missionary would be.

Jim liked for people to know what he believed. He took his Bible with him to school and talked about what the Bible said with his friends. Many people who go to church are afraid to talk about God with their friends or to pray before they eat lunch if other people are watching, but not Jim. He made sure that people knew what he thought.

To go to Wheaton College, which is in Illinois, Jim had to move two thousand miles away from his family and all the things that he was used to. He did not have much money to pay for college, but this did not bother him. His parents had taught him that God would give him the things he needed. Even though he did not know where the money he needed would come from, Jim headed off to college to start getting ready for his future.

Jim was a very serious student. He was an adult now, and he wanted to make the best decisions he could. He was in college to prepare to be a missionary, so he did not want to waste valuable time doing things that had nothing to do with being a missionary. He spent his time studying for classes and reading the Bible and praying. He did not care about football games, basketball games, class picnics, or parties. While most of the other college students found time to do these things and have some fun, Jim thought it was a waste of time. He went to a football game once, just to see why everyone was so interested in it. He had played football in high school, so he knew all about the game. But he did not think college students and adults should be spending their time that way, especially not Christian students. When he heard all the cheering and shouting in the stands, he thought it was foolish to get so excited about something that was not very important. Wouldn't it be better if they used that energy for praising God instead of football players? He would rather stay in his room and pray while everyone else went to the game.

One decision that Jim made was to try out for the wrestling team. This was something new for him, but he thought he could do it. Jim had a good reason for trying to wrestle, and it was not because he thought it would be fun. Instead, he wrestled because it was a good way to stay healthy and build strength for the time in the future when he would be a missionary. Many missionaries live in places where life is rugged and difficult. They have to be in good physical condition to live and work in a place like that. So Jim started wrestling in order to get in shape.

He turned out to be very good at wrestling, even though he had never tried it before. Once, when he was just learning to wrestle, Jim was in a match with a national wrestling champion. No one really expected that Jim would win. When the champion put a hold on Jim, everyone thought the match would soon be over. But he wriggled out of the champion's hold. So the champion put another hold on him. And another one after that. Jim surprised everyone by squirming out of hold after hold. Before long, the champion was embarrassed and frustrated, and he was never able to pin down Jim Elliot. That was the day the rest of the team discovered that Jim was double-jointed and could bend his body in ways that most people couldn't. After that, they called him Rubberneck Elliot.

It must have been fun to frustrate a national champion the

way Jim did, but to Jim, it did not matter if he won or lost the wrestling match, as long as he stayed physically fit.

Jim was very careful about the way he ate, too. In the cafeteria line, he chose his food on the basis of how food could help him be a better missionary. He stayed away from junk food and desserts. Instead, he ate lots of fruit, vegetables, and grains—foods that would help his body stay healthy. He had to be strong and well for the harsh missionary life he wanted.

At the end of his first year of college, Jim was satisfied with what he had accomplished. He had done well in his classes, and that was important. But it was even more important that he had gotten closer to God during that year. He could see that he was making progress toward his goal of becoming a missionary. He had learned a lot, both academically and spiritually. And, he had kept himself in good shape physically.

Jim ended the year the way he had started it—with very little money. After being away from home for nine months, he wanted to see his family. But he could not afford to take a bus or a train. So he hitchhiked. It took him only three days to go two thousand miles. He never waited more than fifteen minutes for a ride, and he got home to Oregon with $1.32 extra in his pocket. To Jim, this was proof that God was taking care of his needs. And this was the God he wanted to serve with his life.

CHAPTER 2

"Glory, brother, what's your verse for today?"

This was Jim Elliot's way of saying good morning when he sat down to breakfast with his classmates. Before breakfast every day, Jim always took time for studying the Bible and praying. This was a very important habit for him. Often he found a verse that he liked especially well, one that he thought would help him during the day. That was his "verse for the day."

Jim believed everyone should start the day with reading the Bible and praying. It was such a beneficial habit; why wouldn't everyone do it? So it was natural for him to think that everyone had a verse for the day. Sometimes Jim embarrassed his classmates because they did not have an answer to his question, and they did not want to admit that they had not read the Bible that day. Some of the students even avoided sitting with Jim for a meal because they did not want him to ask them for a verse.

Jim Elliot was handsome, smart, and friendly. He could have been friends with anyone at the college. In fact, at the end of four years of college, he was very popular. Jim was friendly to everyone, but he was careful about how he chose his best friends.

One of the students who wrestled with Jim on the Wheaton

College team was David Howard. During his first year of college, when he did not get to know many other people, Jim became good friends with Dave. At first, wrestling brought them together. They soon discovered that they had many things in common, especially an interest in becoming missionaries after college. This gave them reasons to do things together other than wrestling. Eventually, Jim and Dave decided to live across the hall from each other in the same dormitory so they could be together as much as they wanted.

Jim and Dave were both involved with a group of college students who were also interested in becoming missionaries. Most of the people that Jim knew best were in this group. They had meetings to learn about becoming missionaries to other countries.

Sometimes these students traveled around to nearby cities and states. They gave talks to groups in churches and schools and explained to other people that many places in the world had no missionaries. The people in those countries did not know that God had made them and loved them and had sent His Son, Jesus, to show the way to God. Jim would get up in front of a room full of strangers, people he had never met before and would probably never see again, and challenge them to think about missionary work. He spoke so convincingly because he really believed what he was saying. Many, many missionaries were needed to go all over the world and tell this good news.

Jim wanted to go to another country and even to a place

far away from any cities. He even thought about going to a place where no missionaries had gone before. The more Jim learned about missionary work, the more he wanted to do this. As he talked to other people, he challenged them to see that they could become missionaries themselves, or they could pray and give money to people who wanted to be missionaries.

Jim concentrated so much on preparing to be a missionary that he was not interested in having a girlfriend while he was in college. He did not go to parties and games and events where men and women students could get to know each other. Many of the girls wanted to go on a date with him, but Jim was not interested. In fact, he stayed away from them on purpose. He thought he could be a better missionary if he did not get married. If he got married, he might be distracted from serving God with his whole heart. The responsibility of a wife and children would be a serious commitment that might take him away from important work. Besides, he wanted to be a missionary in places where it would be difficult to live; it would not be fair to ask a wife to go to a place like that. So Jim did not go out on dates, and he did not think anyone who was serious about being a missionary should. For instance, his friend Dave Howard went out on dates. When Dave came back to the dormitory after an evening out, Jim would say something like, "Have you been out with Phyllis again?" Obviously, he did not approve. In his opinion, Dave was wasting valuable time that he could have spent reading his Bible and praying. How was going on a date going to help him be a better missionary?

David Howard had a sister, Elisabeth, who also attended Wheaton College. She was one year older than Jim and Dave. She was also very interested in becoming a missionary, probably in Africa. Although Jim and Elisabeth had a lot in common, they did not meet until Elisabeth was almost finished with college.

When he met Elisabeth, Jim's world turned upside down. He was not looking for a girlfriend or a wife, but there she was. At first they just saw each other in class. They were both studying Greek so that they could learn to translate the Bible into other languages. During Elisabeth's last semester of college, Jim was in almost all of her classes. Then they started working on their homework together in the library. He had never met a woman like Elisabeth before. She was extremely intelligent— Jim thought maybe she was even smarter than he was. She probed the Bible as deeply as he did, and she had the same intense commitment to serve God that he had, and he admired the way she was trying to do what God wanted her to do, even leaving her family and going to Africa. It did not take Jim long to see that if he was ever going to get married, he would want to marry Elisabeth. He debated what to do and finally decided to tell her the truth about how he felt. Just before she graduated from college and left Wheaton, they went on a picnic with other students planning to be missionaries. Afterward, they stayed behind to clean up and walk back to campus together. Jim told Elisabeth that he loved her, and he could tell that she felt the same way.

But he still did not think that God wanted him to get married. He believed he should be a missionary as a single man. On the one hand, he loved Elisabeth. On the other hand, he did not think he would ever get married. It was hard to figure out why God let him love Elisabeth if He did not want him to get married. But Jim would not do anything that he was not absolutely sure God wanted him to do. And he still believed God wanted him to be a single missionary. Besides, Elisabeth thought God wanted her to go to Africa, and Jim thought God wanted him to go to Latin America. A whole ocean was going to separate them the rest of their lives if they both obeyed God. They could not even think about getting married.

One other student was a special friend of Jim's. His name was Ed McCully. Ed was a leader at the college, class president, an outstanding athlete, and a championship speaker. He even won a national award for a speech he gave. Everyone at the college was impressed by this achievement—everyone except Jim Elliot.

One day, after Ed had won the award, Jim ran into him in the locker room at Wheaton College after a workout. Jim grabbed Ed by the neck and said, "Hey, McCully, so you won the national contest. Great stuff, McCully. You have a lot of talent, don't you? Where'd you get that ability? You know where you got it. God gave it to you. So what are you going to do with it? Spend it on yourself making money for yourself? You have no business doing that. You ought to be a missionary. I'm praying that God will make you one."

Now Ed was planning to be a lawyer, not a missionary. And everyone agreed he would be a great lawyer. But Jim did not let that stop him. He told Ed McCully exactly what he thought.

He did not change Ed's mind, though. Ed went on to law school the next year, while Jim continued his journey toward being a missionary.

CHAPTER 3

When Jim Elliot graduated from Wheaton College, he had no idea what he was going to do next. Most people who finish college try to get a good job and live on their own as adults. Jim's parents and other friends thought he should be a Bible teacher; he had studied the Bible so much over the years that he had become very good at teaching from the Bible. Or he could be a speaker who could talk about missions. If he traveled around the country, they thought, talking to college students, he could convince many people to become missionaries. Maybe these things were even more important than being a missionary himself.

Jim's older brother was already a missionary in Latin America, so Jim could understand that it would be hard for his parents to send another son off to a faraway and dangerous place. But he was determined to go. Too many people in other countries needed to know about God's love. He just could not stay in the United States and live a comfortable life knowing that all those people in other countries did not know God.

The problem was that Jim still did not know where he would go—or when. He was waiting for God to tell him the time and the place. So instead of starting a career after he finished college, Jim moved back to Oregon to live with his parents. He did odd jobs around his church and home, and he spent many hours a day reading stories about other missionaries, studying his Bible, and praying. After awhile, he got a job as a substitute teacher in a high school. Some people thought Jim was being lazy and not even trying to get a real job. But Jim knew that what he was doing was important. Even in these small ways, God was getting Jim ready for what would happen in the future.

About one year after he finished college, Jim attended some special language training in Oklahoma. He spent most of the summer of 1950 learning how to listen to a language that he did not know and writing down the sounds that he heard. Then he would look for patterns in the sounds and form words and sentences. Many languages around the world do not have alphabets that people can write down; the people do not learn to read because their language is never written down. Jim wanted to learn to write down one of these languages so that he could translate the Bible into it. He would learn the language, write it down, and teach people to read their own language. Then they could read the Bible themselves.

The class used missionaries who had already learned a language this way to help the students practice their skills. Jim's helper was a man who had lived in Ecuador and worked with a language called Quichua. There were thousands and thousands of Quichua Indians in Ecuador and very few missionaries. For a long time, Jim had been interested in going to South America. Now he started wondering if he should go to Ecuador. He decided that for ten days he would pray three times a day asking God whether he should go to Ecuador. He had a friend, Bill Cathers, who was also thinking about the same thing, and it was exciting to think that they might be able to go to Ecuador as a team and live among the Quichuas. Going with another man as his partner was exactly what Jim wanted to do.

Something else interested Jim. Near the Quichua area in Ecuador was another tribe, the Aucas. While the Quichuas numbered in the thousands, there were only a few hundred Aucas. The Quichuas had a few missionaries, but the Aucas had none. No one outside their own tribe had ever been able to get close to the Aucas. Some missionaries had learned the Quichua language, but no one had ever been able to get close enough to the Aucas to learn their language. In fact, the Aucas were a violent tribe. They had killed many people who had crossed into their territory. Sometimes they killed people for no reason at all—including people in their own tribe. Even the Quichuas did not feel safe if the Aucas were nearby. It seemed impossible that missionaries could ever reach them.

But reaching such people was exactly what Jim wanted to do. For years, ever since he was a boy, he had been getting ready for the day when God asked him to do something like this—to live in a remote place and reach a group of people with the news of God's love.

After ten days of prayer, Jim decided that God did want him to go to Ecuador. He soon wrote to his parents to tell them of this decision. Jim and his friend Bill Cathers decided to stay in Oklahoma for a few more weeks while they sorted out everything they needed to do to get ready to go to Ecuador. Jim was convinced that he had done the right thing in not getting married—although his feelings for Elisabeth Howard were very strong. Two single men working together was the best kind of team for missionary work.

But things did not work out quite the way Jim hoped. Bill Cathers decided to get married. He still wanted to go to Ecuador, but he would get married first, and he probably would not go to the remote and isolated kind of place that Jim had in mind.

Jim was still convinced that two men working together was the best way to go. But since Bill was getting married, he had to find another partner. That's when he heard that his old friend from college, Ed McCully, had decided to drop out of law school and become a missionary. More than a year had passed since Jim had told Ed that he was praying that God would make him a missionary, but finally his prayers had been answered. Instead of going home to Oregon, Jim traveled to Milwaukee, Wisconsin, to be with Ed and talk about their future.

Ed and Jim decided that they should spend a few months in ministry together in the United States. They went to a small town, Chester, Illinois, and started a Sunday school, visited prisoners, spoke in schools, and produced a radio program. They got along well together and had many of the same goals. It seemed as if they would be a good match for going to

Ecuador together. Jim applied for a passport so he would be ready to leave the United States.

Then Ed McCully decided to get married. First Bill, now Ed. Jim was the only one who still believed that being single was the best thing for a missionary in a primitive place. Like Bill, Ed and his wife still planned to go to Ecuador, and they still wanted to work with Jim. But they were going to take a year of basic medical training first.

So Jim had to start looking for a partner all over again. This time he went back home to Portland to wait for the next step. While he was in Portland, a missionary from Ecuador visited his family. Dr. Tidmarsh had been a missionary among the Quichua Indians, and he and Jim had been writing letters to each other. Because his wife was ill, Dr. Tidmarsh had to leave the work with the Quichuas. He hoped that Jim could come and take over.

Meeting Dr. Tidmarsh in person made Jim even more determined to go to Ecuador—as soon as he could find a partner. He decided to visit a friend in Seattle, Pete Fleming. The Fleming and the Elliot families had known each other for many years. Pete was studying to be a teacher, but he had recently decided that perhaps God wanted him to be a missionary. He was not sure he could really do much good in the world as a teacher, but he could as a missionary. So when Jim Elliot came along and suggested the idea that they should go to Ecuador together, Pete was ready. Although Pete had a girlfriend and was very close to getting married, too, he decided he should stay single, at least for awhile, and go to Ecuador with Jim. Pete made his decision very quickly, and from then on, he and Jim made serious plans to sail for Ecuador in just a few months.

CHAPTER 4

Heat and humidity blasted them in the face on the day that Jim Elliot and Pete Fleming landed in Ecuador. It was February 21, 1952. They had been at sea for eighteen days, and they were excited and anxious to finally be in Ecuador. The port at Guayaquil, Ecuador, was a welcome sight.

They got off the ship and tried to absorb their surroundings—a sea of faces in all directions, store windows displaying a wide variety of goods from sweaters and typewriters to fake shrunken Indian heads. To everyone around them, it was an ordinary day. For Jim and Pete, it was like no other day they had ever lived. The day was the beginning of a future with many questions and challenges.

The first challenge was to figure out where they were supposed to go after getting off the ship. Jim had been sending letters to Dr. Tidmarsh, and they thought he would meet them when the ship came into port. He examined the faces of everyone in the crowd, but he could not spot Dr. Tidmarsh. He was nowhere around, and Jim did not know how to contact him. He and Pete were going to have to do the best they could on their own in a strange place where people did not speak their language.

Using the little bit of Spanish that Jim knew, they found their way to a run-down hotel and tried to get some sleep. But they could not sleep very much. The room was infested with mosquitoes, and it was not long before the two young men were covered with bites. They tossed and turned in the unbearable heat. Jim heard the town clock ring every fifteen minutes all night—along with a braying burro and a dance band. Three days later, he was still scratching from the mosquito bites. This was not exactly the grand beginning to missionary life that he had imagined.

The next morning, things got better. Dr. Tidmarsh arrived, and they had a long talk about the work ahead of them. Dr. Tidmarsh would get Jim and Pete started at Shandia, the mission station where he had been working for many years. Once they were used to the work, he would leave, and they would be on their own. He could visit them for a few days at a time, but his wife's health would not allow them to live in the jungle anymore.

The three of them started their journey by flying to Quito, the capital of Ecuador. Quito was a very old city, set between two mountain ranges. On one side was a smoking volcano. All kinds of people lived in the city—from beggars in rags to rich people in expensive clothes, people pounding cocoa beans with their feet, a boy with a monkey on his head.

As interesting as the city was, Jim had not come there to be a tourist. Quito was a stepping-stone for Jim and Pete. While they were there, their main job was to learn Spanish so that they could go out on their own. Once they learned Spanish, they could move to Shandia. They found a teacher and gathered their books and started to study.

At first, their progress was slow. It was too easy to slip into English because they were with other missionaries a lot of the time. It was natural to speak English. What they needed was to be surrounded by Spanish-speaking people, to be with people who did not speak any English at all. After about two months, they found a room to rent with an Ecuadorian doctor and his family. This plunged them into Spanish all the time, forcing them to speak Spanish and expand their vocabulary. The five children in the house were delighted to correct the mistakes Jim and Pete made. Now their rate of progress was better. They were determined to learn Spanish quickly so they could move on to Quichua territory—one step closer to the Aucas.

One problem made it difficult for Jim to concentrate at times. Although he had not seen Elisabeth Howard for a long time, he still thought of her frequently; and they had been writing letters back and forth. She had not been able to go to Africa, after all. Even though she had been dreaming of Africa for a long time, Elisabeth had decided that God did not want her to go there. Instead, He wanted her to go to Ecuador. So a few weeks after Jim's arrival, Elisabeth arrived in Ecuador, too.

Now Jim wondered if he should ask Elisabeth to marry him. They had both come to Ecuador because they wanted to obey God, not just so they could be together. Perhaps God meant for them to be life partners. But Jim was not ready to get engaged. He still believed that he could be a better missionary to a primitive tribe if he stayed single. It could be years before he could get married. He made no promises to Elisabeth.

Even though Jim and Elisabeth did not make plans to get married, they enjoyed being together. Elisabeth and her missionary partner found a room with a family just across the street from where Jim and Pete were living. The four of them threw themselves into language study as their first priority. The sooner they learned Spanish, the sooner they could move on to jungle work. They studied long and hard hours.

Jim and Elisabeth found time to relax together, too. They took long walks exploring every corner of Quito, seeing the outdoor markets, museums, and craft shops. Once, with a group of friends, they got up at two o'clock in the morning to climb a mountain and watch the sun rise. For the first time since Elisabeth graduated from college, she and Jim could see each other every day and talk as much as they wanted to.

After Jim had been in Ecuador about four months, he had the chance to fly in a plane over the jungle of eastern Ecuador. This is where he eventually wanted to live and work. The plane ride was his first chance to look for some evidence of where the mysterious Auca tribe might be. Since they were not a very big tribe, the Aucas could remain hidden deep in the jungle, and for months at a time no outsiders would see them.

Jim and the other missionaries had heard that the Quichua Indians, a much gentler tribe in the eastern jungle, had had some friendly contact with the Aucas. Normally, the Aucas were known for their brutal treatment of anyone outside their tribe, even other Indian groups. So the possibility that Quichuas were getting along with Aucas was encouraging. But it turned out not to be true. In fact, the truth was that the Aucas had recently killed five Quichuas in that area.

Jim did not spot the Aucas on that trip. But he determined that someday he would find them. Compared to the millions of people in Ecuador and all of South America, the Aucas were a small group and not very important. But to Jim they were important. They knew nothing about the love of God, and he wanted to reach them with this good news. He went back to Quito more determined than ever.

When August came, five months after he arrived in Quito, Jim was ready to move on. His Spanish was very good; some people who heard him talk could not believe that he had been in Ecuador for only five short months. His hard work had paid off.

Elisabeth did not yet know where she would be working. First she had to finish her language study. With excitement and reluctance, Jim said good-bye to Elisabeth and, with Pete, headed for the jungles.

CHAPTER 5

Jim Elliot had never needed a machete before. Now he needed one every day. In Shandia, a good, sharp knife was essential to daily activities.

There were no roads going to Shandia, so Jim and Pete went by air. Only there was no place to land a plane at Shandia, so they had to be dropped off at the nearest little town that had an airstrip, Pano. From there, they hiked through the jungle to Shandia, with a guide using a machete to cut a clean path. The ground was slippery. Sometimes they were up to their knees in mud. They hiked like this for hours, trying to reach Shandia before darkness fell. In the dark, even the guides might not find their way out of the jungle. Just as the moon appeared in the sky, they reached the clearing that was their new home. The Indians gathered around them, curious about the new missionaries. Jim and Pete were relieved to see Dr. Tidmarsh's bamboo home ready and waiting for them.

The next day, they had to go back to Pano for more of their tools and supplies. They did this again and again until they had everything they needed to start working. Without an airstrip, this was the only way to get the things they needed.

Shandia was high on a cliff above the Atun Yaku River. Nearby were the Shandia River and the Napo River. Even though it was a primitive place—without running water or electricity or roads—Jim thought Shandia was beautiful. The birdsongs in the forest enchanted him with their long, low whistles, canary-like tunes, or mellow hoots. At night, he heard the racket of crickets and other insects. The sounds were so fantastic that Jim thought he might record the night sounds for others to hear, from the squeaking bats in the thatched roof to the thundering rapids of the river below the cliff.

Jim and Pete had three main jobs that they needed to do at Shandia. First, they had to learn the Quichua language. When they studied Spanish in Quito, they had a teacher and written textbooks to help them learn. But Quichua was a language that was not written down. They had to learn just by listening to the Indians talk and trying to identify the sounds and words. They carried little notebooks everywhere they went and wrote everything down so they could study their notes more carefully later. Jim's linguistic training from two years earlier was coming in handy now.

Their second job was to build some buildings—houses for missionaries who would join them later, and a school, and a clinic. They hoped that someday Shandia would be an active, thriving center for missionary work. Jim's experience doing odd jobs while living with his parents in Portland was important now. He knew a lot about carpentry.

The third task was to clear a strip of land and make a place where an airplane could land. With their own airstrip, they would be able to get supplies more quickly and without having to make the long, muddy hike to Pano. Jim hired about forty Quichua men to work on clearing the airstrip. He would get them going on the work, and then he and Pete would spend their time in the house studying language. They lived in a simple structure, with boards for the floor and bamboo walls and ceiling. They could look out the windows to see the river, the airstrip, the garden, and even thick forest only a few feet away. It was a nice place to study. The more time they spent on language study, the sooner they would be able to communicate with the Quichuas.

Finding time to study was not as easy as it sounds, though. They were constantly interrupted because the Indians needed help. Neither Jim nor Pete had any medical training, but they had to learn quickly about ways to help the illnesses and injuries of the jungle. Dr. Tidmarsh was a doctor of philosophy and not a medical doctor. But he had years of experience in jungle work and had learned a lot about medicine over the years. Jim and Pete tried to learn as much as they could from him before he left them on their own.

They had a limited supply of drugs, but they learned to use the ones they had properly. Sometimes it would be a sick baby that they took care of. One time, they loaned kerosene to a family so they could keep their lamp going all night while they sat up with the baby. Instead, everyone in the house went to sleep, and the baby died.

Another time, a twelve-year-old girl had been bitten by a snake. When he heard the screaming, Jim scrambled to do what he could; he knew he had to get the poison out of the girl's body before it killed her. He stuck a clean blade on his scalpel and slit her skin to release the venom. But the girl's cries of pain made her family think Jim was hurting her, and they made him stop. Then he tried to suck the snake's venom out of the girl, but she screamed again. It was frustrating to know the best thing to do and not be allowed to do it.

The Quichuas were very superstitious people. If the missionaries could not help them, the Quichuas would call in the witch doctor. He would perform rituals and traditional cures, but really, he was powerless. He could not keep people from getting sick and dying. When this happened, Jim and Pete faced their greatest challenge. Even if they knew what to do, the superstitions of the Quichuas might hold them back, and they would not be allowed to help. What was considered a minor illness in the United States could threaten to kill a child in the jungle, and it was not long before Jim realized that death was a way of life in the jungle. He wrote to his parents on the day that he built his first coffin for a baby born dead, knowing that he would probably have to make many more.

The superstitious way of life among the Quichuas made Jim and Pete work even harder at their language study. If they could teach the Quichuas the truth about God and His power, the Quichuas could be freed from the superstition that ruled their lives. Jim was convinced that the Quichuas needed to learn to read the Bible for themselves so that they could teach their own people. He was determined to open the school that

Dr. Tidmarsh had to close.

The airstrip was finished on September 30, 1952, only a few weeks after their arrival at Shandia. More than 150 Indians gathered to watch as the Piper landed with its load of bread, meat, vegetables, sugar, and lentils. Elisabeth, who was working on the other side of the country, had known that the plane was going, and she made sure there was something special on it for Jim—honey, peanut butter, candy, and crackers. Now at least they could get the supplies they needed to keep working, and food and medicine to stay healthy.

For years, Jim had concentrated on making himself ready for rugged missionary work. He had worked to be in good shape physically and to be close to God spiritually. At last, those years of focusing on the future goal were paying off. Even so, Jim sometimes got discouraged. He had mastered Spanish in only five months. But after three months at Shandia, he still knew almost no Quichua. He had memorized a few practical phrases, but he could not carry on a conversation with his neighbors, much less preach a sermon or teach a Bible lesson. In Quito, his main task was to learn Spanish. But in Shandia, he had little time to learn the language. So many other things took up his time. He could not very well tell the parents of a sick baby that he did not have time to help them because he was too busy studying.

When they had been in the jungle for less than six months, Pete Fleming got sick with malaria and had to fly to Quito for several weeks until he got well. Pete's illness left Jim on his own in Shandia, and now the work went even slower. He felt like he was running from one crisis to another all day long. But he kept at it.

Jim and Pete were carving a place for themselves in the jungle. They learned to swing a machete through the thick vegetation and to eat the foods that were available around them. Jim even learned to eat ants! The young missionaries were also preparing the way for others who would join them. Ed and Marilou McCully were still planning to come to Shandia as soon as they finished studying Spanish in Quito. Then they would have a solid team.

Jim was eager for the future to come. He had not forgotten about the Aucas. Once the work in Shandia was more stable, he still hoped to find the Aucas. Whenever he looked into the jungle, he remembered that the Aucas were out there somewhere. He wanted to find them. And when he found them, he was not going to give up until they knew the truth about God.

CHAPTER 6

The rainy season in the jungles of Ecuador is not something to take lightly. Once the rains begin, people living in the jungle must adjust their activities and wait for the season to end.

In 1953, the rainy season was especially bad—perhaps the worst in thirty years. The projects that Jim Elliot and Pete Fleming had been working on for almost a year came to a stop. It was almost impossible to keep working on construction projects in the rain and mud. Jim and Pete had to stay indoors; all they could do was stand at the window and watch the water come down in thick sheets. Puddles formed in the clearing; then the puddles overflowed with oozing mud. The ground could not absorb another drop of moisture.

Within a few weeks, the weather turned dangerous. The river below the Shandia mission station rose to very high levels, and the cliff above it began to crumble. All the work that Pete and Jim had done for the last year was too close to the water. If the cliff fell, the buildings would fall into the rushing currents. They had no choice but to move the buildings. Even though the rain continued and the mud was knee deep, they got their crew together and started taking apart the house that they had built for Ed and Marilou McCully, who were supposed to arrive in a few months. They rebuilt the house farther from the river.

But the rains kept coming. At the end of July, it rained for four days straight. On the fifth day, they knew there was no escape from the damage the rains would do.

Jim and Pete forced themselves to work on the Quichua dictionary in the morning, despite their worries about the weather. About noon, they looked out and saw that the cliff had begun to break off. Water was surging toward them. They were going to lose their own house within a matter of hours.

Frantically, they packed their equipment and, with the help of a few of the Quichuas, started hauling it to the edge of the jungle, away from the water. In the few hours that they had, they took down the walls, the floor, the window screens —everything they could. These supplies were too valuable to abandon to the raging river. Boxes of food, clothes, papers, and medical supplies were hauled away from the crumbling cliff. While Jim finished up at the house, Pete started on the medical clinic. This was the newest and best of their buildings. Having to tear it down was heart-wrenching, but they had no choice. Pete pulled out cupboards, doors, floor timbers, whatever they could pry loose.

They ran out of time. Jim was pulling out window screens from the house when the front porch gave way and dropped into the river. Jim scrambled to get to higher ground. Within only a few minutes, what was left of the house pitched over the cliff. Jim and Pete watched it go, helpless to stop the heaving force that snatched away in a few moments what had taken them a year to do.

Still the rains came. They kept moving supplies from the buildings that stood closer to the edge of the jungle. Jim lost his shoes in the mud. Now his feet were scratched and cut with every step he took. But he could not stop for his own comfort. For six long, wet, dark hours, they lugged their equipment into the jungle. They lurched through the mud with staggering loads, not knowing how many trips they would be able to make before the river caught up with them.

Chunks of land and trees gave way to the thunderous power of the river. Jim and Pete hardly dared to look behind them to see what they were losing.

Exhausted and having done all they could at three o'clock in the morning, Pete and Jim huddled in some blankets at the home of one of the Quichuas and tried to sleep. After only a couple of hours, one of the Quichuas came running to wake them, shouting about the water. They raced back to the mission station to see that the edge of the water was now only thirty feet from where they had left all their equipment. They would have to move everything again! They cut a trail deeper into the jungle.

By the middle of the morning, the river seemed to level out, and they thought that they were out of danger at last. But so much damage had been done! The McCullys' house, which they already had moved once, was now a few feet from the edge of the broken cliff. Five other buildings, the playing field, and a part of the airstrip were completely gone. A year's worth of work had disappeared.

At her own mission station only a few miles away, Elisabeth Howard was standing by her radio, anxious for news about what was happening at Shandia. She had talked to Jim on the radio two days earlier and knew that the weather was deteriorating and becoming dangerous. After two days of silence, she was worried about what had happened. She tried to find a messenger who would go to find out, but the runners refused to make the trip; it was too hazardous. Finally, she found someone who would go.

Jim sent back a letter that said, "Shandia is no more." Jim and Pete planned to set up a tent for temporary shelter while they sorted out what was left of their mission station. It seemed almost hopeless to think of going on.

When she received Jim's letter, Elisabeth left immediately for Shandia with a group of Indians. Pete and Jim would need all the help they could get.

When the rains let up and it was safe to be on the river, the missionaries had to decide what to do next. Jim and Pete, along with Ed McCully, spent three weeks hiking through the jungle and paddling a canoe on the river to survey the area around Shandia. They visited Quichua villages, estimated how many Quichuas there were, and tried to decide on a new place to build a mission station.

The best spot seemed to be a place called Puyupungu. One of the Quichua Indians who had fifteen children had begged them to come and start a school there. If they tried to go to a village where they had not been invited, it would be very difficult to open a station. But in Puyupungu they would be welcome guests.

Then the question became, who should go to Puyupungu? Ed and Marilou McCully were still studying Spanish and had not yet begun to learn Quichua. They could not start a new mission station from scratch and have any time to learn Quichua. It made more sense for Ed and Marilou to go to Shandia and live in a simple house while they rebuilt that station and studied Quichua. If Pete stayed at Shandia with them, he could help with construction and language study.

That left Jim to go to Puyupungu. But everyone thought it would be best if a married couple worked together to start the school and open a mission station. Jim and Elisabeth had often talked about getting married. They had even gotten engaged, although they had not decided when they would get married. Suddenly, the time was right.

In October of 1953, three months after the flood destroyed Shandia, Jim Elliot and Elisabeth Howard got married. There was no fancy church wedding or satin bridal gown, no guests, no elaborate reception. They got married in a simple ceremony with the McCullys as witnesses. They signed their names in the huge legal register and were declared to be husband and wife.

CHAPTER 7

They were on their knees, but they were not praying. They raised their hands and gestured, but it was not in praise.

Instead, Nate Saint, Ed McCully, and Jim Elliot were on the floor of Nate's house, studying a map of the jungles of eastern Ecuador. It was October of 1955, and they had decided that it was time to begin a serious search for the Auca tribe. They knew they were all living on the edge of Auca territory, yet they could not point to a place on the map and say "That's where the Aucas are." But they thought they were getting close.

Even though they did not know exactly where the Aucas were, the missionaries knew a lot about the tribe. They knew the Aucas were known for being brutal and murdering people for no reason. Not only did Aucas kill outsiders who came into their territory, but they also killed each other. Sometimes two families in the tribe would have an argument and attack each other. Sometimes a whole family would be killed because of an argument.

The Aucas taught their little boys to throw spears accurately and swiftly. For a target they used a figure of a human being; the boys would throw spear after spear until they knew that they could kill someone if they wanted to.

Some people thought that the Aucas might someday

respond to friendship from outsiders. Most people thought that they would just keep on killing anyone who came near them. The missionaries wanted to try to reach them. Jim Elliot learned everything he could about them. He even found a woman, Dayuma, who had left the tribe when she was a girl and who had come to live among the peaceful Quichuas. Dayuma helped Jim to learn some Auca words and phrases. He wrote them down on note cards and carried them with him all the time so he could study them whenever he had a few moments. He learned to say, "I like you." "I want to be your friend." "I want to approach you." "What is your name?" He practiced them over and over again, getting ready for the day when he would speak them to the Aucas.

Nate Saint, the pilot, kept looking for the Aucas from the air. When Nate finally spotted a clearing in the forest and saw that the Aucas were living there, Jim knew the time was coming close that he would meet the Aucas.

They needed a plan, and that's what they were working on in October of 1955. "Operation Auca" began.

They decided first to try to contact the Aucas from the air. They could use Nate Saint's plane and take gifts to the Aucas. Nate rigged a line to the plane that would let them lower a bucket and drop it within reach of the Aucas without having to land the plane. Their first gift was a small aluminum kettle with a lid. Inside it, the missionaries put some bright buttons and ribbons.

They did not see any Aucas that day, but they could see

the clearing in the forest, and they left the kettle there. Later they saw that the kettle was gone; they knew the Aucas had found their gift.

The missionaries all had other work to do; they could not spend all their time looking for the Aucas, although they might have liked to do that. Instead, they decided to fly over the Auca territory once a week and leave a gift.

They chose a new spot for the second gift. The Aucas stayed hidden in the forest—except for one, a man. He peered up into the sky at the plane. Then he went and got two of his friends. Now Nate and Jim and Ed felt sure that the Aucas had picked up the first gift, and these men thought that the plane might leave something else. Their second gift was a machete, something very valuable to a tribe that lived apart from modern civilization.

The next week, Nate had a hard time regaining altitude after dropping the gift. He soon saw that the Aucas had taken hold of the line that the bucket hung from and did not want to let go.

Every week, the Aucas got more curious about what the mysterious plane would bring. More and more of the tribespeople came out of hiding to see the plane.

Jim's turn to ride with Nate came during the fourth week of flights. Once they were in the air, he took out his phrase cards. Using a battery-powered loudspeaker, Jim shouted out in the Auca language, "I like you! I am your friend! You will be given a pot." Then he dropped the pot and waited for the

Aucas to scramble over and get it.

The Aucas no longer were afraid; they were grateful for the gifts and started sending gifts back—a bird, a monkey, food.

A few weeks later, Jim had another chance to fly with Nate. This time he noticed that the Aucas had used the machetes to clear some of the forest, and now their houses were more visible. Jim got ready to drop another machete and a pair of pants. An old man stood beside one house and waved both his arms as if he wanted them to land the plane right there. For years, Jim had yearned to go to the Aucas. Nothing had made him forget about them. He had plenty of work to do at Shandia, teaching and preaching. And now he had a wife and a daughter. But still he wanted to go to the Aucas. He could hardly believe that he was coming close to his dream.

Jim, Ed, and Nate were encouraged by the response that their visits from the air were getting. Before long, they were talking about the next step—contact with the Aucas on the ground. Jim was especially eager to move ahead with their plan.

Ground contact could be very dangerous, they knew. They would not have the safety of an airplane, and they would have to be very careful about what they did. Jim started writing out plans, step-by-step.

Jim, Ed, and Nate were all planning to be part of Operation Auca. But they wanted to include some other people, too. Roger Youderian was a missionary who had worked with two tribes in Ecuador, and he was interested in Operation Auca. And Pete Fleming, Jim's partner in the early Shandia days, was interested. So the team would have five members.

Together the team had to decide their next step. Nate thought that they should continue with their flights and dropping gifts, perhaps doing it more often. Ed thought they should concentrate on finding a place where they could clear an airstrip to land the plane. Jim wanted to do something soon. If they went into Auca territory with canoes, they would not have to wait to clear an airstrip. Pete was not sure the time was right; the Aucas were very dangerous, and the missionaries should move slowly. While they pondered what to do next, they continued their weekly flights.

By now, the Aucas had figured out that the plane came every seven days, and they stood in the clearings looking for the plane. Nate was confident enough to fly the plane closer to the ground now. He could look into the faces of the Aucas and see their friendly expressions. The Aucas were not afraid of the missionaries. Should the missionaries be afraid of the Aucas?

As they began to plan their next step, the missionaries tried to think of everything that might happen. They could go in and set up a temporary camp along the river and wait for the Aucas to come to them. If they sensed any danger, they would leave immediately. They knew the Aucas could turn on them without warning, and they were experts with spears. What would the missionaries do then?

They decided to take guns with them—but only to frighten

wild animals. They would not shoot at the Aucas. They would not use guns to save their lives. But then, no one thought that the Aucas were going to hurt them.

Everybody would have a job. Nate found a place on the beach where he thought he could land the plane, so they would not have to go by canoe. They called the place Palm Beach. Jim would be in charge of constructing a tree house for the team, so they would be out of reach of animals at night. Roger made up the first-aid kit, and Ed collected items that they could trade with the Aucas. Pete would fly in and out of Palm Beach with Nate each day taking supplies.

They were ready.

CHAPTER 8

They set the date for January 3, 1956. If they did not go then, they would have to wait until after the rainy season. The rainy season would last several months, and during that time it would be difficult to travel or to live for a few days on the beach without a real building to stay in. No one wanted to wait several more months, so the men made their plans to go to Palm Beach right after the holidays. At Christmastime, when several missionary families were together, they made their final decisions about what they would do to contact the Aucas on the ground.

Jim was not sure that Pete Fleming should go to Palm Beach. Pete was Jim's first partner, and Jim respected Pete. And Pete wanted to find the Aucas as much as anyone. But Jim thought Pete might be too valuable to risk, especially because he had learned Quichua. Jim was thinking about the work at Shandia and Puyupungu. If Pete joined the team and then something happened, all the men who could speak Quichua would be lost. This would be a major setback to the missionary work among the Quichuas.

Ed McCully jumped in, objecting to Jim's idea. Ed had a wife and two little boys, and his wife was pregnant with their third child. He told everyone that if he thought anything dangerous was going to happen to them, he would not be going. If Pete wanted to go, he should go. In the end, Nate said that he really needed Pete's help. Ed, Jim, and Roger would stay on the beach. Pete and Nate would fly in with supplies each morning, spend the day, then fly out before dark. Pete decided to go.

The men had decided what they were going to do. Their wives still had to decide how they felt about Operation Auca. Even though Ed had convinced the men that they had no reason to be afraid, the women knew that what their husbands were doing was risky. They had their own quiet conversations about what might happen.

The day came for Jim to fly from Shandia to Arajuno, the place that they were using as a base for Operation Auca. Elisabeth helped him pack his things, including items that might help entertain the Aucas and give the men time to show their friendship. Jim took a harmonica, a View-Master with pictures, and a yo-yo, as well as some practical things, like a snakebite kit, a flashlight, and his Auca language cards. Today was the day he had been waiting for; he was going to the Aucas. He felt as ready as he could be, and he had no doubt that this was the right thing to do.

As Jim headed out of the house toward the plane, Elisabeth held her tongue. If Jim had any sense of danger, he did not show it, and she tried not to show how she felt. She wanted to say, "Do you realize you may never open that door again?" But she didn't. She simply walked out to the plane with him, where Jim kissed her good-bye as if he would be back in a few hours. He hopped in next to the pilot and waved good-bye. Elisabeth stood on the lonely airstrip and watched the plane disappear from view as the sound of its engine grew faint.

That night, the five men gathered in Arajuno: Ed McCully, Nate Saint, Roger Youderian, Pete Fleming, and Jim Elliot. They had to get down to the details that would make their plan work. They stayed up late trying to think of everything that might happen so they could be ready for it. Every movement they would make the next day had to be planned out in detail. Nate would have to make several trips from Arajuno to Palm Beach. They made lists of all the equipment they would take with them on each trip and double-checked to make sure everything was working. Certain items would go in first so they could build a shelter. Less important items would follow on later trips. Nate could fly only during daylight hours, so they had to make sure they had everything they needed at Palm Beach before dark.

After hours of planning, the details were in place. They were as ready as they were ever going to be. No one slept much that night as they waited for the dawn.

In the morning, the plan called for Ed and Nate to make the first flight at eight o'clock. At the last minute, the plane had a problem with the brake fluid. Nate was an excellent mechanic as well as a pilot, so he fixed the problem, and they took off right on time. The sky was foggy that morning, which made it hard to spot the beach where they wanted to land. But just as they approached the beach, the fog thinned out, and they could see where they were going.

Nate flew over the beach one time to make sure he knew where he wanted to land and looked for any objects that might damage the small plane. The beach seemed clear; it would be safe to land the plane. He set it down precisely between two trees and brought it to a halt.

From the air, Ed and Nate could see trees and other obstacles, but they could not be sure what the sand would be like. Now they found out that it was soft—too soft. As they came to a stop at the river's edge, they felt the plane sink into the sand. For a moment, their stomachs were in their throats. The plane could flip over and be ruined; they would be stranded on the beach. But the sand held. It was just firm enough to keep the plane from flipping over.

Ecstatic finally to be on Palm Beach, Nate and Ed jumped out, unloaded their equipment, and ran up and down the beach looking for things that might cause problems later.

After a few minutes of clearing the beach, it was time for Nate to take off again. He needed to be able to get the plane going at a fast speed on the ground before lifting into the air. But the sand was too soft; the plane's wheels would not move. Aware that precious minutes were ticking away, Ed and Nate leaned on the plane with all their weight and pushed it back, away from the water and into some bushes. The ground was firmer here, but Nate would not have as much room as he wanted for taking off. For a few stressful minutes, he did not know if he could take off at all. But his first try was successful, and he was on his way back to Arajuno.

Ed McCully was alone on the Auca beach, unarmed and exposed to threats from wild animals or unfriendly Aucas.

On the second flight, Nate took Roger and Jim to Palm Beach. Now there were three men on the beach. On the third trip, Nate took in the radio, some tools, and the basics Jim needed to start work on the tree house. Jim organized the men as they worked, and that night they slept thirty-five feet off the ground, safe from whatever might prowl around the base of the tree.

Jim wrote a note to Elisabeth that night for Nate to take to her the next day. He wrote about the mosquitoes and the beauty of the jungle. His words were hopeful; he was excited that perhaps the next day would be the day that they would reach the Aucas at last. Being on Palm Beach in close range of the Aucas was the dream he had been waiting for.

The waiting began. The men were settled on the beach, Nate and Pete were flying in and out every day, and radio contact with Marj Saint at Shell Mera was clear. They were ready. But where were the Aucas? The men felt sure they were being watched, and the gifts they left on the beach were picked up during the dark nights, but they never actually saw any Aucas.

Once, just as they landed, Nate and Pete saw clear human footprints near the beach—and not just one or two. Not sure whether to believe the footprints were human, Jim Elliot ran downstream along the beach to inspect them close up. He found footprints of various sizes—proof that the Aucas had been nearby within the last few days.

They had to keep waiting. With their camp set up, they did not have much to do to pass the time. Jim read aloud from a novel, and they floated in the river water to try to get away from the heat and the bugs.

The third day on the beach began just as the first two. Pete and Nate flew in early in the morning to spend the day with the team on Palm Beach. The men took turns standing along the river and shouting Auca phrases into the jungle. If the Aucas were as near as the missionaries thought, they could come out at any moment. Jim and the others used every friendly, encouraging phrase they had learned in the Auca language.

Suddenly, a male voice answered one of their calls! Although they had been hoping for an answer, they were still surprised when it came. Three Aucas stepped out of the trees and into clear view, a young man and two women. They wore no clothes, but they had strings tied around their waists, wrists, and legs. They also had wooden plugs stuck through holes in their earlobes.

The five missionaries jumped to their feet, instantly alert. They called out, "*Puinani!* Welcome!" The Aucas stood on the opposite side of the river, examining the strange outsiders, who looked so odd, yet spoke familiar words.

The Auca man started to talk, but the missionaries could not understand him. They did not know very many words, and he was talking too fast. They had been practicing speaking Auca phrases, but that was not the same as hearing an Auca speak the language. So the missionaries tried "talking" without words; they started watching what the man did with his hands instead of just listening to his voice.

Suddenly, Jim pulled off his shirt and pants and plunged into the water. He understood what they wanted! They wanted someone to help them across the river, and he was going to do it. He was not going to miss this chance to get close to the Aucas, not after waiting so long to get to this point.

The other missionaries called out to Jim to be careful. If he got into trouble in the middle of the river, they would not be able to help him. And once he got to the other side, the

Aucas might decide to attack, and there would be no one to protect him. For a fraction of a second, Jim slowed down and glanced over his shoulder at his friends. Then he kept going. He did not think he would be attacked. It seemed to him that the three Aucas wanted to be friends. All he had to do was convince them that he wanted to be friends, too.

Once Jim was on the way, one of the women cautiously stepped off a log on the other side and into the water, followed by the man and the other woman. Jim offered his hand, and the young woman took it. He led them safely across the river. His mind pounded with the thought that he was actually touching an Auca! He had spoken Auca words, and they had understood him. He was sure they were responding to his friendship.

Once back on the other side, Jim scrambled to get out his language cards. He wanted to tell the Aucas that they had nothing to be afraid of.

He managed to get this idea across, and the Aucas relaxed. All three of them started talking. They did not seem to notice that the missionaries did not understand them.

The missionaries had come prepared with gifts—knives, machetes, a model airplane. One of the women was fascinated by a copy of a magazine. They also got out their cameras and starting snapping pictures. The Aucas did not seem to mind, although they did not know what a camera was.

The three Indians were curious and friendly. The missionaries gave them names. The man was George, and the younger woman was Delilah. And the missionaries kept talking with their hands.

Delilah walked over to the plane and started to inspect it. She had never seen a plane close up. She rubbed herself against it, then stretched her arms out to the side to playfully swoop as she had seen it do.

George was soon beside her. But he had not come across the river just to look and touch. He had bigger plans. George pointed and gestured until the missionaries realized that he wanted a ride in the plane. He showed them how he would call out to the people below as he had seen the missionaries do.

Jim and the others looked at each other. They had not expected this, and they were not sure what to do. They quickly decided to let him fly. George was no danger to them. Why shouldn't they do what he asked? George could help their work a lot and help them to meet the leaders of his tribe. Besides, George was ready to go, and it did not look like he would change his mind.

Finally, Nate climbed in beside George and started the engine.

George paid no attention to Nate. Instead, he leaned out the opening next to him to see where he had come from. He saw his village below and yelled and waved to his people. He was pleased with his achievement. Who else in his tribe could claim such an experience?

The missionaries had thought out how they would

communicate their needs to the Aucas. Once George was back on the ground, they gathered around him. Someone stuck sticks in the sand to represent trees, then pulled out a small model of the plane. They showed how the plane could not land on the ground because of too many trees. Then they took away some of the sticks and showed how the plane could land easily in a clear space. The look in George's eyes told them that he understood: The missionaries could not fly to his village because of the trees. But if the Aucas would take out some of the trees, then the plane could come to his people.

This kind of sign language went on all afternoon as the Aucas tried out all the little gadgets the missionaries had with them—rubber bands, balloons, yo-yos. The men even fixed lemonade and hamburgers for their guests. Jim felt that they were really making contact. He hoped that George might invite them to his village. But so far George did not seem interested in that.

Nate and Pete had to leave before dark, so they gathered up all the film everyone had used and the notes they had taken. They wanted to be sure these things got to a safe place. Before climbing up into their tree house, Jim, Ed, and Roger offered their kitchen shack to the Aucas for shelter. Delilah was not interested and wandered into the forest. After a few minutes, George followed her. The older woman stayed on the beach, tending a fire most of the night. But in the morning she was gone. A ring of smoldering coals was the only evidence of her presence.

And the waiting began again. Jim and the rest of the team had no way to know if George would come back or if others from the village would come. Their excitement swelled as they thought about reaching a tribe deep in the Ecuador jungle, people who had never seen a church, never read a book, never sung a hymn, never heard a missionary preach. But they had to keep waiting. Hour after hour they waited on the beach, grasping at activities to keep themselves busy.

In the middle of that long, quiet day, Jim grew restless and impatient. "I give them five minutes," he said to the others. "If they don't show up, I'm going over." His common sense returned, though, and he did not go. It was so hard to wait and not be able to do anything more to reach his goal.

Finally, two days after George and the woman had visited, Nate got restless and took the plane up during the day to check around. He flew over the village. There were only a few women and children walking around the clearing. Where were the men? A moment later, he saw them. They were marching as a group toward the beach. Swiftly, he turned the plane around and returned to the beach. He jumped out, shouting, "This is it, guys! They're on the way!" The others put down their books and got ready to meet an official welcoming committee of Aucas.

Nate got on the radio to communicate with his wife. It was 12:30. Excitedly, he told Marj about the approaching men and promised to radio again at 4:30 with news of the meeting.

Standing on the beach waiting for the Auca men to arrive,

Jim Elliot had no regrets about being the first one to wade into the river two days earlier. He knew that years of patient preparation were about to be rewarded. He had waited a long time for this day.

CHAPTER 10

Promptly at 4:30, Marj Saint was at the radio waiting for contact from her husband. Pete Fleming's wife, Olive, had been ill and was recuperating at Shell Mera. Together, they huddled at the radio waiting for the familiar crackle that would mean their husbands were at the other end. But the radio was silent. Marj checked her watch to make sure she had the time right. She did. They watched the clock as 4:30 passed, then 4:45, then 5:00.

Nate Saint was a stickler about communication. To him, staying in radio contact frequently and regularly was a rule that should never be broken. He always let Marj know where he was and what his condition was. He never, ever forgot. So why did he not call this time?

Marj and Olive speculated that perhaps the radio on the beach had broken down since Nate's last call. But Marj was not satisfied with that explanation. The men had planned for the possibility that the radio might fail; there were two radios on the beach. If one was not working, Nate would use the other one. That was no explanation. Silence could not be good news.

Soon it was too dark to expect that Nate and Pete could fly back that night as they had been doing. Marj turned off the radio.

Marj and Olive passed the evening with routine activities

and did not alarm any of the other missionary wives or the guests at Shell Mera. But they did not sleep much. Finally, the long night passed. In the morning, Marj and Olive came face-to-face with the reality that they had feared during the dark hours of lying awake. There was still no word from Nate.

Johnny Keenan, another missionary pilot, took a plane up and flew over the area where Operation Auca was based. Within a few minutes, he was on the radio with Marj—with bad news. He had spotted Nate's plane, stripped of all its yellow fabric and not in any condition to be flown. He saw no sign of the five men, but the damage to the plane—along with Nate's silence—clearly meant something was wrong.

Now Marj called the other wives. Barbara Youderian and Marilou McCully came in from Arajuno. Elisabeth Elliot arrived from Shandia, along with Rachel Saint, Nate's sister. They gathered in Marj's spacious, comfortable home, fearful of what had brought them together. Obviously, the men had fallen into danger—but just what had happened? Nearly everyone was hopeful that at least some of the men had survived and would be able to tell them the whole story. Marilou McCully was so convinced of this that she did not stay at Shell Mera with the others; she went back to her house at Arajuno. Since her house was the closest to where the men had gone, they would go there first when they came out of Auca territory. She wanted to be home when they arrived.

Another day passed. By now, word had gone out around

the world that the five missionaries were missing.

On the third day, Johnny Keenan flew over the river again. This time he spotted a body floating in the river. From the air, it was hard to tell who it was, and Johnny did not dare try to land and retrieve the body. But it meant that at least one of the men had not survived. The women, holding their small children in their arms, all looked at each other, knowing that at least one of them was now a widow. Fear for the well-being of all their husbands multiplied.

Three days of silence dimmed the hopes that anyone had survived. Marilou McCully had waited patiently at Arajuno, but no one had come.

On the fourth day, the Air Force Rescue Operation joined the search that a network of missionaries and Quichuas had started. Now searchers could cover more territory in a shorter amount of time. The air force also could give protection to the searchers on the ground, in case someone was still alive.

The wives kept waiting, taking care of their young children and passing one hour at a time.

Finally, someone sent for Marilou McCully to come back to Shell Mera. The women braced themselves for the news that the searchers brought.

Four bodies had been spotted from the air, and the Quichuas on the ground had found the fifth. The bodies had not been identified, but there were five. No one had survived. There was no information on what had happened, and no way to find out what had provoked the attack when every sign was that the Aucas were responding to the missionaries' friendship.

The Aucas themselves retreated into the jungle, once again beyond reach.

With their husbands gone, each of the women had to decide whether she would stay in Ecuador or return to the United States. Marilou McCully decided to return to the States for the birth of her third son. Later, she returned to set up a home for missionary children who attended school in Quito. Olive Fleming helped Marilou set up the school and then returned to the States permanently. Barbara Youderian returned to work with the Jivaros, the tribe she and Roger had worked with before. Marj Saint took up a new job in Quito. Elisabeth Elliot returned to Shandia, where she continued working with Rachel Saint.

Rachel was studying the Auca language with Dayuma, the young woman who had helped Jim Elliot learn key phrases of friendship. Shortly after the killings at Palm Beach, Rachel Saint showed Dayuma photographs of "George" and "Delilah" and the other woman. The men had taken a camera to the beach and used it before their deaths. Now Dayuma got excited. She recognized the older woman as her own aunt and the younger woman as her cousin. Dayuma had left the Aucas because of a brutal family feud. She had never been sure whether any of her family was still alive. Knowing that her aunt and cousin were alive gave her hope that others in her family had survived. This information made her think that perhaps she could go back to her own people after years of living among the Quichuas.

Because of those photos, Dayuma became a bridge between outsiders and her own people. Elisabeth and Rachel had already decided to take up where the men left off and try to reach the Aucas. Without Dayuma, it might have been impossible for the missionaries to continue any contact with the tribe. Friendship did not happen right away, but eventually, the Aucas started responding to the missionaries again.

Elisabeth and Jim Elliot had talked about going to live among the Aucas as a family someday, and Elisabeth was still willing to do this. She took her young daughter, Valerie, and moved to the Auca village. Rachel Saint, Nate's sister, went with her. Once they were settled there, they could do more intensive language study and eventually present Christianity to the Aucas. Dayuma continued to help them, and she herself became a Christian. While she lived among the tribe, Elisabeth collected information about that day on Palm Beach, trying to find out just what happened to Jim and the others— and why.

Elisabeth left the Auca work after a few years and returned to live in the United States. Rachel Saint stayed on with the Aucas for many years. Eventually, many of the Aucas became Christians. Rachel nurtured the church, which was led by some of the same men who had killed her brother and the others. The tribe was now known as the Waorani, which was their own name for themselves. "Auca" was a Quichua word that meant savagery. Now that they were Christians, the tribe did not want the world to know them by their old reputation. Rachel and other missionaries worked for many years to put the Waorani language in a written form—just as Jim Elliot had wanted to do. They looked forward to having the Bible in Waorani.

More than thirty years after the killings, Olive Fleming returned to the scene. She had remarried about two years after Pete's death and now traveled to Ecuador with her husband and the youngest of their three children. Unlike thirty-three years earlier, it was now perfectly safe for Olive and her family to visit Palm Beach.

Except for one flight over the watery grave with the other widows, Olive had never seen Palm Beach. Now she sat where the men had built their shelter, although the beach had changed over the years. Even the tree that had once held the tree house thirty-five feet off the ground had been wrenched out of the ground by high water.

One of the Waorani women, Dawa, started speaking. Rachel Saint translated for Olive and the others.

Dawa told about that day long ago. She had seen what happened from a hiding place in the forest. The missionaries had not used their guns to defend themselves. They had decided before they ever went to Palm Beach that they would not fire on the Aucas, and when the time came, they stood by their decision. They fired into the air, trying to frighten their attackers, but they let the Waorani kill them.

Rachel Saint had heard this story before. But Dawa went on with something Rachel had never heard before. Dawa told how, on the day that George and the others had visited the beach, one of the men had taken something out of his pocket to show them. In 1956, the Aucas did not wear clothing and did not understand what a pocket was. It seemed to them that the man was taking something out of his body. What he took out was a photograph of Dayuma. The missionaries had carried the photo in hopes that the Aucas would recognize Dayuma and know that she was still alive. But just as they did not understand pockets, the Aucas did not understand photography. They did recognize Dayuma, but what had happened to her? What had the strangers done to Dayuma to make her flat and small? How could Dayuma come out of the man's body? How had she gotten in there? The obvious conclusion was that the man had eaten Dayuma.

When the three visitors told this story to the rest of the tribe, fear spread that the missionaries wanted to eat the whole group.

And so the Aucas killed the missionaries.

Kimo, a Waorani Christian leader, now joined Dawa's story. He and Dawa, with the others hiding in the jungle during the attack, had looked over the top of the trees and seen what looked like "a hundred flashlights." At the time they did not understand what they were seeing. Later, when they had become Christians, they knew they had seen angels and heard them singing. Dawa told Rachel that it was the vision on the beach that first persuaded her to believe in God, and Dawa had become the first Christian in the tribe five years later.

Rachel Saint was as surprised by this information as Olive Fleming Liefeld was. She had lived among these people a long time. Why had she not heard this story before? No one can say why Dawa did not tell her story sooner.

Jim Elliot, along with Pete, Ed, Roger, and Nate, gave his life trying to reach the Aucas. At the time, it might have seemed that they failed. But thirty-three years later, a once savage tribe was living peacefully with its neighbors and teaching the Christian faith. According to Dawa and Kimo, it all started with a vision on the beach when the men were killed.

Three years after Olive's visit to Palm Beach, and thirty-six years after the deaths of the men, the Waoranis celebrated having the entire New Testament in their own language—the work Jim Elliot had hoped to do. Although his part in the dream was not what he thought it would be, Jim Elliot's dream of a lifetime had been fulfilled.

Key Dates in the Life of Jim Elliot

October 1927

Jim Elliot is born in Oregon.

September 1945

Jim enters Wheaton College in Wheaton, Illinois.

May 1948

Jim and Elisabeth realize they love each other.

June 1948

Elisabeth graduates from college and leaves
Wheaton.

Spring 1949

Jim challenges Ed McCully to be a missionary.

June 1949

Jim graduates from Wheaton and returns to Portland,
Oregon.

Summer 1950

Jim attends linguistic training in Oklahoma; Bill
Cathers and David Howard get married; Jim commits to going to Ecuador.

Fall 1950

Ed McCully decides to leave law school and consider missionary work.

January 1951

Jim begins ministry in Chester, Illinois, with Ed
McCully.

June 1951

> Ed McCully gets married; Jim returns to Oregon.

February 1952

> Jim and Pete Fleming arrive in Ecuador.

April 1952

> Elisabeth arrives in Ecuador.

August 1952

> Jim and Pete finish language study and go to the
> Shandia mission station.

December 1952

> Ed and Marilou McCully arrive in Ecuador.

July 1953

> Flood at Shandia destroys a year's work.

October 1953

> Jim and Elisabeth get married in Quito; they move to
> Puyupungu to establish a new station.

June 1954

> Jim and Elisabeth move to Shandia.

February 1955

> Jim and Elisabeth's daughter, Valerie, is born at
> Shell Mera.

September 1955

> Nate Saint and Ed McCully see the Aucas for the
> first time.

October 1955

> Search for Aucas begins in earnest; first gift drop made.

December 1955

Plans finalized for ground contact with Aucas.

January 3, 1956

The missionaries land on Palm Beach and set up camp.

January 6, 1956

George, Delilah, and another woman come to the beach.

January 8, 1956

Last radio contact with Marj Saint at Shell Mera.

If you enjoyed

GOD'S AMBASSADORS,

check out these other great
Backpack Books!

GIRLS' CLASSICS
Including *Pocahontas,*
Little Women,
Pollyanna, and *Heidi*

BIBLE HEROINES
Including *Deborah, Ruth,*
Esther, and *Mary*

MODERN HEROES
Including *Corrie ten Boom,*
Eric Liddell, Billy Graham,
and *Luis Palau*

BIBLE HEROES
Including
Noah, Joseph,
David, and *Daniel*

CHRISTIAN ADVENTURES
Including *Ben-Hur,*
The Pilgrim's Progress,
Robinson Crusoe, and
The Swiss Family Robinson

AMERICAN HEROES
Including
Roger Williams,
Abraham Lincoln,
Harriet Tubman,
and *Clara Barton*

THE SON OF GOD
Including *Jesus,*
The Miracles of Jesus,
The Parables of Jesus,
and *The Twelve Disciples*

Great reading at a great price—only $3.97 each!

Available wherever books are sold.
Or order from
Barbour Publishing, Inc.
P.O. Box 719
Uhrichsville, Ohio 44683